Finding Home

Finding Home

My Journey from
Post-War Germany to America

Brigitte D. Moore

Soul Attitude Press

Map of Poland by s.radek
Used under license: GFDL ver. 1.2 or CC-by-sa ver. 2.5, 2.0, and 1.0

Visit the author's website for more information:
brigittedmoore.wordpress.com

Soul Attitude Press - Pinellas Park, FL
www.soulattitudepress.com

Printed in the United States of America

First Edition

ISBN 978-1-939181-39-8

For my grandsons Christopher and Thomas Moore

And in memory of my parents Doris and Hans Grunwald

Plunge boldly into the thick of life,
And seize it where you will,
It is always interesting.

~ Johann Wolfgang von Goethe

Contents

Poland after WWII

Part of Germany before 1945

Wrocław was formerly Breslau

Szczecin

Gdańsk

Poznań

WARSZAWA

Łódź

Wrocław

Kraków

Białystok

Brześć

Lublin

Wilno

Baranowicze

1947 border

Curzon line "B"

Lwów

Stanisławów

Part of Poland before 1945

INTRODUCTION

World War II and its aftermath affected the lives of millions. My family was not exempt. We left our hometown of Breslau in January 1945, armed with one suitcase. There was no room for any kind of keepsake. For months we drifted from town to town, until at last we were offered asylum in the small town of Mügeln, located in the state of Saxony. Difficult years followed. My mother fought for our survival, aided by her American cousins, who sent us packages with food and clothing.

At the end of World War II, Germany was divided into East and West. It was our bad fortune to land in East Germany under Russian Communist rule. Our hardships continued. Those fortunate enough to live in the West benefited from the Marshall Plan, through which the United States gave monetary support to help rebuild Europe. Introduced in April 1948, it ran for four years. As a result, West Germany became prosperous. The Soviet Union early on withdrew from participation, thus ensuring that East Germany did not thrive.

After my father was interrogated by East German Secret Police on several occasions, he felt it was time for us to escape to the West. In the spring of 1951 our family journeyed to West Berlin. To avoid being caught, my father left first, my brother Peter and I followed, and a few days later my mother and sisters joined us in West Berlin. Once again, a small suitcase carried just a change of clothes.

Throughout these years we were always known as "Flüchtlinge" (refugees) no matter where we lived. I felt I did not belong anywhere.

When I chose to immigrate to the United States in 1958 I frowned upon everything German. I was angry that my childhood and teenage years had been stolen from me. And when I learned of the atrocities committed by Hitler and his regime, I felt a deep shame. I also did not care to own any kind of memorabilia for fear that they would be taken from me.

In time I came to terms with these feelings and the day arrived when I could honor my German heritage. I still have family in Germany and love when I can visit. I also remember the first time I took delight in a small antique dish that was given to me. It became a cherished treasure.

Mostly self-educated, my love for culture and reading helped me to master the English language. I am still fluent in German, but now prefer to write in English. Because the first twenty-one years of my life are my most vivid memories, I wanted to record them. I did this first for myself as an exercise and at a later time thought that my grandsons, Christopher and Thomas, should know their German grandmother's (they call me Oma) story. Thankfully they are growing up in a free country. Perhaps my writing will help them appreciate how privileged they are.

Lastly, I also dedicate these words to the memory of my parents, Doris and Hans Grunwald, without whose courage and perseverance I would not be who I am today.

What I have written is not only a record of my difficult childhood, but an illustration of how those trying years provided fuel that gave me the strength and determination to pursue the seemingly impossible goal of moving to America. Life propels us ever forward. There is no going back. My hometown of Breslau is now under Polish rule and is called Wroclaw. Breslau may be where I had my beginnings, but America is where I am at home.

Breslau - Losing Home

Years before I was born ominous clouds hung over Germany. World War I had taken a severe toll on life and created monetary hardships for the German people. Thus it was no surprise that someone like Adolf Hitler would become the leader of the Nationalist Party as early as 1921. His stronghold was mainly in the province of Bavaria. There he and his cohorts created havoc in local beer halls. In September of 1930 the Nazi party became the second strongest political party in Germany. Still, no one took Hitler seriously, particularly the intelligentsia and military aristocracy. He was considered a joke, an Austrian housepainter! Nevertheless, in January of 1933 Hitler became German Chancellor. He would soon reveal himself a madman.

It was into this hotbed of fanaticism and mania that I was born on February 10, 1937 in the beautiful 12th century city of Breslau, the capital of Silesia. Breslau was situated on the Oder River which flows 562 miles from Czechoslovakia to the Baltic Sea; known for its outstanding University, ancient churches and old architectural buildings, Breslau was a cultural center of Eastern Germany. My memories of Breslau are vague, but in my mind's eye I see beautiful old buildings and landmarks. The city's real beauty was not revealed to me until much later, in books and old postcards I inherited.

I was given the name Doris Herta Brigitte. Because my mother answered to the name of Doris (her name was Dorothea), my parents decided to call me Brigitte, the name I still go by. Gitti and Gittchen were "Kosenamen" (endearments) my mother occasionally used.

My father was Hans Grunwald. He was tall and lean; in his

youth he had a full head of dark, curly hair, which began to thin when he reached his forties. He had a sonorous voice and once sang the part of tenor in an all male choir. Vati (Daddy) loved animals. I remember a bright green parakeet he trained to sit on his shoulder. The bird's name was Petey and I was charmed when Petey jabbered into my father's ear.

When I was born his father and two sisters were no longer alive. He studied business and worked as a sales representative for a Metal and Steel company. Since metal and steel were important to the war effort, Vati was spared serving in the German Army. However, in the spring of 1944 he could no longer escape the draft. He was forty-one and the father of four children.

My paternal grandmother was slight in build. I'm also petite and seem to favor her in body type. She wore her grey hair curled into a small bun at the nape of her neck and she dressed in dark colors, the fashion for older women of her generation. She had a strong faith, drawn from her Lutheran upbringing. I can still recite two short prayers she taught us; one said before meals and the other at bedtime. She became a widow at a young age and raised my father and his two sisters with the help of her mother. Both sisters died at an early age, Herta when she was twenty-one and little Lotte when only five years old.

My mother gave the appearance of being much taller than her five foot two inches because of her proud carriage. She wore her rich auburn hair shoulder length, and before we became refugees, she was always beautifully coiffed. She dressed with great care and took pride in her appearance. Mutti (Mommy), had beautifully shaped legs, which looked especially good when she wore high heels. There was a spring to her step, making it seem as if she was always in a hurry to get some place. I remember her as being even-tempered, smiling often, and loving life. From stories she told us, she was quite a rebel in her youth. She lost her father when she was just sixteen and insisted on wearing white to his funeral, even though black attire was the norm in those days. Her high spirits served her well when faced with the hardships of the after-war years.

My mother's maiden name was Helweg. According to her, no one has this name unless they are a relative. Before I was born, Mutti , lost her only brother Walther in a tragic train accident. It was said that Onkel (uncle) Walther, a doctor, played Chopin without ever having had piano lessons. My mother's younger sister, Felicitas whom we called Tante (aunt) Fee, was our only close relative. She and my mother were estranged while we lived in Breslau so I did not meet her until after the war. She had one son, my cousin Bodo.

My maternal grandmother, Oma Helweg, had a substantial build. She was Catholic and so was my half-brother, Hannsjoachim (Hajo for short), whom she raised. Her grey hair framed her face and was cut short on the side. Like my paternal grandmother, she too wore a small bun at the nape of her neck. Oma Helweg had difficulty with her legs, which were swollen. She needed the help of a cane to walk.

My mother's skills with thread and needle were nonexistent. Whenever Oma Helweg visited there would be a large basket filled with socks and other clothing items waiting for her in the living room. She would sit in a comfortable chair near the window while her hands were busy sewing on buttons and darning socks. I looked forward to Oma Helweg's visits because she was a wonderful story teller. I would perch on a little stool by her side and beg for story after story.

Oma Helweg lived near the lovely Scheidniger Park where we children would chase after red squirrels. The only thing I remember about her apartment is that she had a large balcony that looked like a greenhouse. She must have had a green thumb, as plants and flowers of many varieties grew there in colorful pots. There even was an old bathtub filled with rich, dark earth where garland-type plants weaved themselves along the screens.

My best memories are of Bohrauerstrasse 5, where our family lived in a large apartment on the third floor of a building close to the Hauptbahnhof (main railroad station). I remember huge wooden doors at the entrance. A tunnel led to a courtyard, and another building was behind it. It was called "Hinterhaus," (the house in the back). Because of its location, it was not as desirable as the one in front. In my mind's eye I can still see all the rooms and furnishings of our apartment, and that's where they will remain because the building was destroyed toward the end of the war.

The large hall at the heart of the apartment was often used for raucous games of catch. Towards the front was a large dining room and our father's study. The kitchen faced the back.

The Kinderzimmer (children's room) was at an angle next to the kitchen. Long and narrow, it eventually housed four of us. From the Kinderzimmer one entered a narrow hall. A bathroom was to the left, and in the back was my parent's bedroom. All the rooms had beautiful porcelain Kachelöfen (tile ovens) that kept us warm during cold winters. They required quite a bit of work, as each had to be fired up with wood and coal. In wintertime, after we returned from the frigid outdoors, we would warm our cold feet on the hot tiles.

Vati's study was also where my parent's went to relax in the evening. In addition to Vati's large desk, it was furnished with a divan where my mother reclined to read. There were shelves that held knick-knacks, a radio, and a large round table with two comfortable chairs next to it. My father's high-back desk chair had a beautifully carved crown at the top. The chair created problems for him when he was taken prisoner of war by the Russians. When they found a picture of the chair in his pocket, they thought Vati came from nobility. He had a hard time convincing them that he was just an ordinary citizen.

Two narrow glass doors opened up to a balcony just large enough to stand on. It faced the street. There are two scenes that remain imbedded in my mind involving that balcony. In one, two Hitler Youth members drag a boy between them. He was on his knees and they forcefully pulled him along the sidewalk. I remember thinking how much that must have hurt. The spectacle upset me. In the other scene, my parents are looking toward the viaduct leading from the railroad station. Several cattle cars were just sitting there. My Mother and Father talked in a conspiratorial way. I could not hear what they said. I just knew that something sinister was taking place. I felt weird and lost as nobody explained anything.

Our dining room was only used on holidays and Sundays. We children had our main meal at lunch time in the kitchen. I remember eating a lot of Semolina made palatable with condensed fruit juice or fruit when in season. During the cold winter months our mother fed us a tablespoon of cod-liver oil, guaranteed to keep us healthy. I dreaded it when she reached for the dark brown bottle, kept in the pantry. I would close my eyes and scrunch up my face as the awful tasting liquid went down my throat.

My mother told me that I broke my collarbone when just a toddler. Evidently I was put in a large cast that made me fall a lot. I also remember having the mumps. In those days people tied a wool scarf around the head to keep the cheeks warm. I see myself sitting in bed looking like a rabbit.

In addition to my half-brother, Hannsjoachim, twelve years my senior and being raised by my maternal grandmother, I had three other siblings: My brother, Peter who was two years older than I, and my two sisters, Bärbel and Uschi (the diminutive of Ursula), five years and three and three-quarter years younger than I.

When I was little we spent a lot of time in the Kinderzimmer. My brother Peter instigated and led many wild games. As the only boy – and the oldest – he probably wanted to show off. He took great joy in dropping things from the window into the courtyard, and then running downstairs to retrieve them. Unfortunately, someone would invariably pick them up before he got there. Thus, my mother lost valuable spools of thread and Peter lost a few of his tin soldiers.

When Peter was barely six years old he wanted an adventure. He packed his small Rucksack (backpack) with a change of clothes, got hold of the family's ration cards and disappeared. I can't remember how long he was gone. The police brought him back and when asked why he ran away, he replied, "I wanted to see the world." Soon after this incident my parents took Peter to a Children's Clinic to be examined by a Psychiatrist. I remember sitting in a waiting room for what seemed like an eternity, fretting over my brother. The outcome was less than satisfactory. My parents were told that my brother would either be a genius or land in the gutter. How ridiculous!

During the warm summer months an organ grinder would often play in the courtyard between the two apartment buildings. The repetitive sound of the organ bounced off the walls and soon everyone was leaning out of their windows, including us children. The organ grinder was dressed in a long black coat in spite of the warm weather. A bowler type hat sat on his head. He seemed to have difficulty cranking the handle of his music box, which interrupted the smooth flow of the music. Even so, I was enthralled, loving the unusual sound of the organ. When people began to drop coins wrapped in newspaper, I begged my mother for some. Peter and I would struggle to see who would throw the coins from the window. He always won.

When Hitler came to power he decreed that at age eighteen all young males and females serve in the Reich Labor Service. Girls were assigned to work in agriculture or in homes. Boys did manual and agricultural work, and then were drafted into the army. This was mandatory. Thus we often had a young girl working in our home. She helped my mother take care of us children – taking us to the park – watching us when Mutti had to be away from home. I don't remember anyone in particular, but there were several girls; most were nice.

During this time, because so many of our family had died before we children were born, we saw few relatives. I recall visiting Oma Grunwald in her apartment. On one particular visit my brother Peter and I were allowed to ride a streetcar by ourselves; we were just eight and six. That made me feel quite grown up. The conductor wore a dark navy uniform, and a shiny contraption was strapped around his middle. This is how he made change. The various sized coins fit into different slots. Peter teased me and said he would not pay for me. That brought me close to tears. I should have known that he was joking.

Oma's apartment was tiny, but exuded warmth and coziness. She made us drink a concoction of raw eggs, beaten with sugar and some other ingredient. This was guaranteed to make us healthy and strong. I always was very obedient and somehow managed to choke it down. Peter was less obliging. He only drank it when Oma told him that it would make him grow.

On September 1, 1939, Hitler invaded Poland, marking the beginning of World War II. I'm not sure when the air raids began, but I can still hear the sirens that announced them and sounded when all was clear. I believe Russian bombers flew over Breslau on their way to strategic targets in the West.

We children were often torn from our beds in the middle of the night. My parents would come to our room to wake my brother and me so we could get dressed while they tended to my younger sisters. I climbed right back into bed because I was so sleepy and Vati had to rouse me again and again. The basement was dank and hardly had room for everyone. Many of our neighbors brought their own stools to sit on. A bare light bulb dangled from the ceiling, throwing ominous shadows on grey walls. Here we huddled on a narrow bench until the all-clear sounded. My teeth rattled and I shook from the cold—or fright. Mutti was busy comforting my sisters. When Vati placed a warm blanket around my shoulders, I felt grateful. Everyone was nervous except Peter. He bounced around pointing his finger to the ceiling while making shooting noises. I worried that a bomb might hit our house. Would we be buried under the rubble? In time these nightly excursions became a way of life.

My memories of starting first grade in 1943 are vague: A festive breakfast was served in our dining-room; my backpack sitting on a chair, my Zuckertüte (a large cone filled with candy and small favors) was to sweeten my first day of school. First grade remains mostly a blank. Only one scene is still vivid: We were learning to read and I was not doing it well enough. The old, white haired teacher called me to the front of the room. She had me hold out my hands as she whipped them with a bamboo stick. This not only hurt, but I felt totally humiliated.

The year was 1944 and the German Army was suffering defeats and tremendous losses on all fronts. No one escaped the draft as young and old were now conscripted. And so my father was drafted as a common soldier. He left for basic training. My half-brother, Hannsjoachim, who was a student at University, was deployed as "Luftwaffenhelfer" (child soldiers), as whole school classes of male students had to serve in the air force.

Around this time school children were evacuated to outlying villages as constant air raids interrupted the learning process. My brother Peter was sent to a Kinderheim (children's home). Mutti was relieved when she found out that one of the caregivers was a young woman who used to work in our home. She felt that Peter would get extra good care.

And so my turn arrived when my class of twenty little girls, just seven years old, was ordered to evacuate to the country. Our teacher accompanied us to ensure the continuity of our lessons. Mutti packed a small suitcase for me, all the while chatting away, making light of this event that she knew frightened me. She told me the village was not far away and that she would come to visit.

On the day of our departure we walked to the nearby railroad station where we met with my classmates. Suitcases were lined up on the platform like a row of ducks. These would later be loaded into the baggage car by porters. All the girls clutched their mothers' hand. Some cried quietly. I kept looking into Mutti's face, hoping she would say I did not have to go.

Our teacher arrived, followed by a porter who carried her huge, weathered suitcase. It was decorated with colorful stickers, attesting to the fact that she had once been a world traveler. She wore a huge hat that hid her stern face. Waving a black umbrella, she tried to get our attention: "Kinder, Kinder." But no one listened.

Once the train pulled into the station we could no longer escape our destiny. Our mothers prodded us up the steps where porters waited to assign us to two reserved compartments. My classmates and I pushed to get close to the window so we could wave goodbye. It was a heartbreaking scene. As the train left the station our mothers vigorously waved white handkerchiefs until we no longer could see them. The handkerchiefs fluttered like white doves about to take flight. I craned my neck out the window until the platform disappeared and with it my mother.

Our teacher was in the next compartment. From time to time she poked her head into ours to make sure we were well behaved. At first there was total silence. No one felt like speaking. In the end our curiosity won out; we discussed what life might be like in the country. Our nervous laughter hid how we really felt – terribly frightened.

I remember getting off the train, trembling as I stood in that strange small train station. And I remember clutching my doll that Mutti insisted I bring, when this roly-poly man with a balding head pointed to me and said, "I want that girl with the big bow in her hair." He turned out to be the mayor of the village, a widower who owned a small farm with cows and horses, and a butcher shop. His widowed sister ran his household. I had hit the jackpot.

The school was right across the street from the mayor's house. Though I missed my family, I was relatively happy for a time. I was treated with kindness, maybe even love. The mayor's sister asked to be called Frau Anna and she and I shared a room facing the courtyard of the farm. I felt comforted that I had her company during the dark nights, as I had never slept alone.

The silence of the village felt strange. The only noise came in the early morning hours when roosters crowed and cows mooed. Farm life agreed with me. I took delight in the large outdoor cat named Alexander. He was jet black with just a little white around his nose. It was his job to hunt for mice, and to my horror he dropped a dead one in front of my feet one afternoon. I screamed and ran into the house.

There was a chicken coop and I helped Frau Anna collect eggs the hens had laid. The cows had to be milked morning and evening and I was fascinated how their fat udders yielded buckets of milk. I remarked how I would like a nice cold drink of milk right from the cows. Frau Anna laughed and explained that the milk was actually quite warm.

The mayor and his sister gave me a lot of attention and I was content and happy. That is, until the mayor decided to marry a widow from Breslau. The wedding took place in a small country church. A reception followed right after at the mayor's house. My classmates and teacher were invited. We had to learn songs and poems which we performed after the ceremony. Mine had something to do with cooking, for I held several wooden spoons in my hand.

Frau Anna was no longer needed and returned to her home. Things changed dramatically. The new lady of the house was not fond of children and treated me harshly. One time I wanted to help during the milking of the cows. I struggled to carry a heavy bucket to the house. A small amount of milk spilled. The wicked witch (in my mind she impersonated a witch), slapped my face. All joy left me and I began to long for my home, my mother and siblings.

In late November of 1944 Mutti arrived unannounced for a visit. She found me sitting alone in the large restaurant room, a bowl of soup in front of me. Tears ran down my face, dripping slowly into the bowl. Mutti was quick to take in this scene and announced on the spot that I was coming back home with her. This was fortuitous as in January of 1945 we were forced to flee Breslau and none of the other parents were able to get their children. Railroad connections had been cut off.

Home was no longer the same. I missed my father's presence and Peter's adventurous spirit. Even so, it felt good to be home. And then my sister Bärbel contracted scarlet fever. My father's study became her sickroom and only Mutti was allowed to enter. Antibiotics had not yet been discovered and her recovery was slow. There was little to entertain her except for a few toys and picture books.

Oma Grunwald came to help. I would soon be eight, and felt important when I was sent on errands to the bakery and a nearby store for groceries. I also spent much time with my sister Uschi, barely three years old. She was a sweet and sunny child and I loved to listen to her innocent chatter. Mutti was preoccupied with caring for a sick child and supervising the running of her household. Life was not easy.

Christmas approached, the last we would spend in Breslau. I

don't know how Mutti managed to get a Christmas tree into our living room without us noticing it. As in previous years, the living room was off limits the week before Christmas. Our grandmothers arrived to help us celebrate Christmas Eve. When Mutti tried to open the connecting door that led from the study to the living room, she found the key hole blocked with coins. Bärbel, in her boredom, had found a form of entertainment.

It would be Bärbel's first time out of quarantine. Mutti carried her through the other door and held her in her arms so she could look at the lit Christmas tree. The tree was a beautiful sight and we all felt the wonder of this special night even though sadness hovered in the air.

Throughout World War II, Hitler used powerful, rousing classical music to make important radio announcements to the public. Works by Wagner, Grieg, Sibelius and Liszt were favored and I can still hear one particular piece, Franz Liszt's, "Les Preludes". This piece played when on January 19, 1945 the announcement came over the radio ordering all women and children under sixteen to leave the city.

Hitler had decreed that Breslau would be a Festung (fortress) to be defended at all cost when the Red Army came close. The siege of Breslau raged for three months. Ninety percent of the city was destroyed and 30,000 soldiers and civilians lost their lives. Much of the destruction was made by Germans who did not want the enemy to take over any part of the city.

Mutti began to make preparations. I can still see her taking the measure of each room in our apartment – a silent farewell. While I was too young to realize it, my mother understood that we would never return to the life we once knew. She took our bird Petey to a neighbor who was staying. Other residents rolled up expensive Persian carpets and other treasures to store in the basement. My grandmothers arrived at our apartment looking forlorn, each carrying a small bag. They had come to join us, but we were leaving without my brother Peter. I felt so lucky to be home and not still in the village with my other classmates.

We walked to the railroad station with a stroller and a small suitcase that held some clothes, hardly enough to keep us going for long. It was bitter cold, one of the coldest winters on record. We learned later that many people who had left their homes on foot had perished. An immense square faced the railroad building. People were squatting on bundles, boxes or suitcases. Most were refugees from further East. Their stoic expressions frightened me. Everyone spoke in hushed voices.

The doors to the station were locked, admitting no one. My mother found a spot where we could rest and told us to wait there. She disappeared through a side door. Not long after she returned wearing a Red Cross armband. She shepherded us into the station through that same side door. Inside chaos ruled; women, children, soldiers, bundles, boxes and suitcases were crowding the platform. We squeezed our way into this medley of bodies and belongings. There were no train schedules; no one knew when a train might come.

Mutti was worried. How would she manage to get us onto a train should one arrive? My maternal grandmother walked with two canes and my paternal grandmother was frail. They would not be able to help her with the luggage and my two small sisters. There was no sense of time. When a train did pull in, pandemonium broke loose. The excitable crowd pushed themselves towards open train doors.

Out of nowhere a young soldier appeared. He helped my mother to get everyone into the train. Miraculously, we all landed in one compartment. Others joined us until no seats were left. The narrow walkways were jammed with suitcases and people, the restrooms blocked. The train sat for a long time, but at last the huffing and puffing began. First slowly and then more rapidly, the train went in a westerly direction.

No one spoke. Everyone was glad to have found a seat. Sometime during the ride I had to go to the bathroom. The restrooms were locked and to my great embarrassment a lady pulled out a cooking pot into which I relieved myself. Someone opened the window and poured out my warm urine, which gave off steam. The train moved ever so slowly and stopped several times.

Oma Helweg decided that she wanted to get off in the town of Gleiwitz where she had friends. She felt that this journey would prove to be too difficult for her. Mutti could not convince her to stay with us. We hugged and kissed her, not knowing that we would never see her again.

When the train stopped in Dresden, the capital of the state of Saxony, we were told to disembark. Red Cross workers, all women in their traditional uniforms, attempted to bring order to the multitudes gathered on the platform. We were herded from the station onto waiting buses, which transported us to a public school that had been set up to house refugees. Straw mats were spread on the floors and each family was assigned an area. We received a meal of hot soup and bread. Evening had arrived and there was little to do but go to sleep. I can't imagine what went on in my mother's and grandmother's minds, but children do live in the moment and we were asleep in no time.

Breslau train station

Anna Grunwald (paternal grandmother), left;
my father, back, left; Herta and Lotte, front

Ottilie Helweg

Oma Helweg and Hajo

Me, Bärbel, Uschi, Peter, Mutti - 1942

Mutti, Vati and Bärbel - 1942

Vati in his study

Seeking Refuge

In January of 1945 Dresden could not handle the large number of refugees who had poured into this beautiful old city. Efforts were made to move many of us to outlying towns. I don't remember how many days we spent in Dresden before we boarded another train which took us to the small town of Nerchau. Here, local people came to the railroad station and picked whom they wanted to put up in their home. I don't think they had a choice. The government ordered everyone who had an extra room to take someone in.

A charming lady invited my mother and little sisters to stay with her. She was a middle-aged woman whose husband was serving in the war. Frau Schulte had lost a son in the war and was happy to have company. She took special delight in my sisters. My grandmother went to another family and someone else took me. I have a dark memory of the family that invited me to their home. My mother told me later that once she was settled she managed to convince her landlady to take me in as well. According to her, I slept in the basement on top of an old bathtub filled with coal.

The most controversial raid of World War II was the bombing of Dresden on February 13, 1945, when Allied bombs rained on this beautiful city. The seventh largest city in Germany, Dresden was a center of culture and architectural wonders. At the time of the bombing it was filled to the breaking point with refugees. Other than undermining the morale of the German army even further, there was no sane reason for this horrendous attack. Much has been written about the ensuing inferno when Dresden burned for days. It is not my place to make a judgment, I'm only glad that we were moved to another location, or we might have perished with 30,000 others. We could see Dresden burn from the distance. Smoke and flames filled the sky for days. The raid took place on my mother's birthday and three days prior I had turned eight. There were no celebrations, no birthday cake, no presents; just gratitude for being alive.

As refugees we received assistance from the local government. Each week my mother collected some money to help with expenses, but there was little to buy. Stores were empty and food was scarce. At a Red Cross Office we were able to get clothes to augment the few garments we had brought from home. Wherever my mother went, we went. Holding my sisters' hands, one on each side, I either lead the way or trailed behind. Everything took time and we stood for hours in long lines. I don't recall how else we passed the time. There was no school for me, but I had always been my mother's helper and so I welcomed any chore she would give me.

At last the drab, cold winter came to an end. Spring was in the air and soon trees and bushes burst forth with new life. Birds sang and chirped away and all kinds of insects appeared, seemingly from nowhere. We children were delighted to be outdoors for longer periods of time, inventing games that kept us occupied. I'm not sure when the "Maikäfer" (June bug) appeared. What fun they were. I have never seen them in this country, but they must exist somewhere. They were large, and they had a heavy brown shell; their wings made loud noises when we trapped them in cardboard boxes. To keep them alive we punched holes all over the box and gave them leaves for nourishment.

There was talk about the war coming to an end. We heard gunfire in the distance. It was difficult to know what to believe, as news was sketchy and Germany had not yet surrendered. There were huge warehouses in the area where the government had stored food and many other commodities. They did not want the enemy to find these caches and allowed the local populace access to these treasures. Naturally my mother went along as people streamed to the various locations. She managed to secure a Leiterwagen (wagon with rails at the side), reminiscent of those that farmers used. She returned with large bags of sugar, flour, salt, items of clothing and I can't remember what else. She became proficient in bartering with others for items we needed.

I accompanied her on one of these outings when a warehouse holding bolts of material was opened. The pushing, noisy crowds scared me. As soon as the doors opened, people streamed into the warehouse, not caring if they stepped on each other. They behaved like animals. Mutti and I were able to get several bolts of beautiful material in vibrant colors and fanciful designs; a feast for the eyes.

I sometimes wondered how my mother coped. There was no news about our father or brother Peter. The fate of her mother was also unknown. Mutti had filed missing person reports with the Red Cross who worked ceaselessly to help locate loved ones

In late April the US and Russian armies met at the Elbe River, which was close by. We heard gunfire. Everyone was scared. What would happen when the enemy arrived?

We did not have a long wait. First the Americans came. Tanks slowly made their way down the narrow streets. The soldiers appeared friendly and threw candy bars, which everyone fought over. I was not brave enough to obtain one. I saw my first African American on one of the tanks. He was very black, but had a beautiful smile and he did not scare me.

We did not know why the Americans withdrew. The next to arrive were the Russians. With them entered Poles and Czechs. The picture now became grim. They were not friendly, and who could blame them. They had suffered so many atrocities by Germans throughout the war.

They invaded homes and took whatever hit their fancy. Rape of young girls and women of all ages was rampant. Adults gathered in groups, whispering about horrible events that they didn't want the children to hear. Whenever possible, families hid young girls in attics or basements. My mother was defiant and wherever she went she flanked herself with her three girls. The victorious armies never molested us.

On May 7, 1945 the German Army surrendered, and VE day arrived on May 8. At first nothing changed. People had been on ration cards for so long, it came as no surprise that rationing would continue. Food became even more scarce and money was worthless.

Toward the end of May an ex-German soldier convinced some of the refugees in the area to attempt to go back to their hometowns. Everyone dreamt about returning to their homes and soon a group of thirty people formed, willing to make this trek on foot. There was still no news about any of our family members and so my mother decided to go along. We took the little wagon and loaded it with all we had accumulated. The bales of material took up most of the space.

Early one morning, the group assembled at the designated meeting place. We were an unlikely collection of women of varied ages, a few men, and a handful of children. Some had bicycles they rolled and would occasionally ride. My grandmother came with us. She and I took turns pushing or pulling the wagon. My sisters' legs tired easily and sometimes they sat on top of the wagon.

We walked like ducks along the side of country roads. The pace was slow. Luckily the weather was friendly. We stopped often to rest. There was no traffic, only an occasional farmer broke the monotony of deserted roads. We relieved ourselves in the bushes, being careful to grant each other privacy. I can't remember how many miles we walked that first day. In the evening we reached a small village, and our leader tried to find a farmer who would put us up for the night. We were offered a barn, but no food. This particular village had been badly plundered and had nothing to share with us.

One incident remains indelibly printed in my memory as if it happened yesterday. We were walking through a forest, and the dark mood of the night before had lifted. Conversation was lively as people chatted amiably. There even was some joking going on. And then shots could be heard in the distance. Everyone froze. Far off, a lone soldier, carrying a machine gun, was gesturing for us to halt. I was so scared and began to tremble. Soon tears ran down my face, but before I could have a good cry, Mutti slapped me hard, telling me to stop. She was afraid for my safety and didn't want to give the soldier reason to become annoyed. I learned to be brave, to not show my emotions; a lesson I've found hard to break.

The soldier was Polish, wearing a Russian uniform. Looting was forbidden and he was covering his tracks. No words were spoken as he pointed to his wrist and fingers, indicating that he wanted watches and other jewelry. My mother wore shoulder length hair. She had sewn her watch and rings into a wide velvet ribbon she used to tie back her hair. Mutti made no move to hand over her few treasures, whereas most others were quick to hand over their watches and rings.

The soldier was just pointing to our little wagon, wanting us to unload it, when suddenly he heard a noise in the distance. This made him skittish. He grabbed one of the bikes and disappeared into the woods. Not a word was spoken for some time. Everyone was glad that our ordeal was over and that no one had gotten hurt.

We were no longer at war; we had become a defeated nation. This truly hit home when we entered the city of Torgau where we hoped to make railroad connections. A dark cloud hung over this town—store windows were boarded up, houses were in ruins and rubble lay strewn on every street. There was an absence of color, an absence of hope, an absence of joy. We were so very tired from walking and longed for a bed, a change of clothes. Hunger had become our companion.

Our leader attempted to communicate with anyone of authority. He learned that there were no railroad connections going east. Though no one knew this as yet, our part of Eastern Germany would soon be assigned to Poland. We were told to give up our journey. Our group dispersed and everyone went to fend for themselves.

My mother was my hero again as she fought her way through this depressing and ravaged town. She located the local "Wohnungsamt" (an office that assigned living quarters), which placed us into a furnished apartment above a jewelry store. Here we collapsed, too tired to look around, just glad to have a place to rest.

The apartment was devoid of any personal belongings. It felt cold and deserted. Perhaps the previous occupants went to the

West to escape the arrival of the Red Army. We discovered a garden in the back of the building that had not been tended in a long time. Nevertheless, it was a refuge from the dismal look of the streets.

The jewelry store below still functioned. Poles, who were stationed across the street in barrack-like buildings, kept the owner busy. They wanted him to make lots of wristwatches from big alarm clocks; at least this is what he told us. We watched Polish women struggling to ride bicycles. One in particular got my attention. She wore a fur hat, though it was no longer cold. What a wonderful time she had, laughing, weaving all over the road. A soldier held onto her seat and ran with her.

Spring was turning into summer and since nothing could be accomplished by staying in this town, Mutti wanted to return to Nerchau, where she hoped to find news about our father, brother and her mother. We boarded yet another train and though it had taken us three days on foot when we left Nerchau, our return trip took hardly any time. Upon disembarking from the train we were told that Nerchau had an outbreak of typhoid and was no longer accepting refugees. Somehow Mutti was able to convince the authorities to let her check with Frau Schulte to see if she had news from our family. Once again good fortune was on our side.

A German soldier had come to Mrs. Schulte's house with my brother Peter. He volunteered to take my brother to Breslau when he found out that we were no longer at this address and on our way to our former home. Luckily, Mrs. Schulte didn't think this a good idea. She told him to return Peter to the place where he had been staying. Upon learning this news, Mutti and Oma Grunwald departed immediately on foot to fetch Peter, while Mrs. Schulte watched us girls.

We were joyful to have Peter back in the family fold. These good feelings were dampened, however, by the fact that Peter was in miserable shape. He was severely undernourished.

Mügeln - the After-War Years

Adrift and without a place to stay, Mutti was advised to go the town of Mügeln. There we found ourselves on Main Street with our meager belongings. My brother was so weak he had to drag himself from stoop to stoop. For the first time, I saw my mother break down in tears, when out of nowhere a stout woman with a kind face stopped to talk with her. She used soothing words and patted her back. She invited all of us to her apartment, where she served us a warm meal. We spent the night in makeshift beds. The next day we were directed to a deserted factory on the outskirts of town where a makeshift camp had been set up for refugees. Here we settled in until more suitable lodgings could be found.

We slept on straw mats strewn on concrete floors. Cooking took place outdoors on little stoves fashioned from bricks we found in back of the factory. Luckily it was summer and the days were mild and beautiful. My sisters and I entertained ourselves by exploring the spacious grounds of the factory where we played hide-and-seek. We also built intricate structures from the many bricks lying around.

My brother was sick; he was listless and unable to keep anything in his stomach. A young local doctor and his wife came to our makeshift camp to give Peter medical attention. Each day they brought special food and tenderly spoon-fed him. It did not take long for Peter to regain his strength. Eventually, to our relief, he returned to being his old lively self.

We were not the only displaced persons who had found lodging in this cold, barren factory. Many came from East Prussia and they spoke with strange accents. They were farmers from rural areas and we had little in common with them.

Because of the lack of sanitation and the crowded conditions, it did not take long before our long hair became infested with lice. Nothing was available to rid ourselves from these horrible pests. Mutti put up a good fight as she combed our long hair with a special comb, but it was hopeless. A nurse who visited recommended that our heads be shaved. First my long braids were cut off and then the nurse used a sharp razor to shave my head. I was unable to utter a single word, feeling so humiliated; a scarf covered up my shame. Some of the older boys in the camp delighted in pulling the scarf from my head. They sang a silly song I can still remember. It had to do with a bald man who just had a little fringe of hair.

Before winter set in we moved to new quarters. A low-lying shack that had once served as a tool shed became our new home. In spite of the primitive lodgings, Mutti could hardly contain her happiness! At last we had a place of our own. Oma found a furnished room that suited her just fine. She visited with us often, helping Mutti when she had to be away from home.

The one-room shed did not even have a floor; hard-packed dirt would provide little warmth during the harsh winter month. The shed was long and narrow. An ugly brown burlap covering went half-way up the walls. To the left was a double bed where Mutti and my sisters slept. Two narrow single beds were on the other side, butted against each other, where Peter and I slept. A table and chairs and a small chest of drawers completed the furnishings provided for us. Our few garments hung on hooks as there was no closet. In the center of the room a black, iron stove with several tiers served for heat in the winter months. It was also the only way Mutti could cook our meals. We needed coal and firewood to make it work. A stone slab on one side of the shed held a sink with cold running water.

There was no bathroom. Instead a wooden latrine in the entranceway served as our toilet. There was no running water for flushing and toilet paper was hard to get. But, thankfully, we did not have to go outdoors.

Next to the latrine, the owner boarded a sheep in a small stable.

My brother took great pleasure in leading the poor animal to our living quarters where he attempted to ride it. From sheer fright, the sheep often dropped little pellets on the floor, which my brother made me clean up.

A door at the end of the room led into a sunken storage area. Here we stored our meager supplies. It was also where Mutti would do our wash, using the large vat that sat in the center on raised bricks. A fire needed to be lit underneath to heat the water.

In the beginning we could only give ourselves a sponge bath until Mutti obtained a round metal tub. Even with the tub, bathing was a time-consuming and laborious event. It took a long time to heat enough water to fill the tub. We took turns sitting in the cramped space, washing ourselves as best as we could. Bathing was especially difficult when winter arrived. No one wanted to take off their clothes.

During these trying months of 1945, my sister Uschi's sunny disposition brought a measure of cheer to our lives. Her delightful laugh lit up her pretty face and I never tired of looking at her during those moments. When winter arrived, Mutti called her "mein Wärmeöfchen" (little warm stove) because her body gave off so much heat during the bitter cold nights. Uschi and my sister Bärbel were only fifteen months apart, giving the impression that they were twins. They were wonderful company for each other.

For my sister Bärbel, the lice continued to be a problem. She had scratched her head incessantly, which caused ugly open sores on her scalp. The lice laid their nasty little eggs underneath the infected scabs. A Lutheran parish nurse came several times a week to clean out the infection. She used alcohol and tweezers to get underneath the scabs, a painful procedure which caused Bärbel much pain. Her screams invaded my dreams.

I remember most that we were always hungry. Food could only be bought with ration cards. The shelves in stores were mostly bare. When a delivery arrived, long queues formed. I took turns with my mother to stand in line.

The locals supplemented their supplies by going to the forest for firewood, mushrooms and berries. My mother, having been bred in a large city, befriended women who could show her what to do in the forest. I went with her on these trips. The road to the forest led up a steep hill. We pulled our trusty little wagon to hold our harvest. One was only allowed to pick branches that had broken off. No one was permitted to cut down live trees. The small amounts of firewood we collected did not last long.

Mushroom picking was best after a nice rain when they popped out of the ground like magic. Mutti and I each carried a basket. The local women showed us which mushrooms were poisonous. I loved mushroom picking. Each mushroom had to be inspected. I learned to differentiate between good and bad. The variety was amazing; best were the Steinpilze (stone mushrooms) because they were big, fat and meaty. At home Mutti used some mushrooms to add flavor to our tasteless soups. The rest we sliced and threaded on thin twine to dry for later use.

We went to the forest at least twice a week. One time my mother sent Peter and me to collect a load of wood. As soon as we got out of town he told me to go on by myself. My sense of duty spurred me on and I managed to find my way. I was frightened in the dark and lonely forest! What I brought home was pathetic, but my mother thanked me nevertheless.

Peter and I were enrolled in school. I dreaded meeting other children. My hair had started to grow in, but it would be a long time before I would have my braids back.

I was placed into the third grade according to my age, skipping second grade entirely. It was not difficult to get back to learning. I loved history, geography, music and German. I was less fond of mathematics. I learned that the following year I would be taught Russian, which became mandatory as of the fourth grade. I looked forward to learning a foreign language. During music lessons we not only learned German folksongs, but also Russian songs; many of them were of a patriotic nature. It did not matter to me. Although my voice was not special, I loved to sing.

After school many of my classmates congregated in front of the local bakery. The aroma of freshly baked bread wafted from the open door. A discussion ensued as to who would go into the store to beg for a slice of bread. One day it was my turn. I was mortified and felt like running away, but since I had shared in these meager morsels, I had little choice.

It took time to get used to the Saxonian dialect spoken by most of the children and teachers in school. There was a sing-song quality to their inflections and they pronounced words that began with the letter "K" by substituting it with a "G". This amused Peter and me. We copied their way of speaking, laughing hysterically. But we were careful not to let anyone hear us for fear of reprisals. Peter got into many fights with local boys. I think he was taunted and tried to defend himself. This continued for several years. He often walked around with a black eye and bruises. I abhorred all violence and was greatly upset when Peter got into these fights.

Vati was alive! We received notice from the Red Cross that he had been taken prisoner of war by the Russians. He was somewhere in Russia. Mutti felt consoled. It would be many months until Vati could send us a personal message. When the first one arrived, we read it over and over until the brown craft paper became brittle. My father had beautiful handwriting. He used the smallest script to fit as many words as possible onto this square card that was just a little larger than a postcard.

Vati wrote how after his hospitalization he was ordered to connect with his battalion on the Eastern front. But there no longer was an organized army. The war was coming to an end and he hooked up with other soldiers who decided to return to their homes. They obtained civilian clothes from a local farmer. While attempting to return to Breslau, Vati was captured by the Russians and declared a prisoner of war. He was briefly detained in Breslau. There he had the chance to see our apartment building, which had been destroyed, and he feared that we had been killed. His relief was great when he learned that we were safe.

As soon as we heard from Vati my mother sat down to write him a letter. She wrote in large letters. Peter and I urged her to make them smaller so more news could fit on the fragile onion skin pages. The Russians allowed their prisoners to write one post card per month, but we were not sure if Vati ever received our letters.

Winter arrived with a vengeance. It was so cold that our supply of coal and wood dwindled quickly. We spent a lot of time in bed underneath featherbeds, with socks on our feet and mittens covering our hands. By morning ice had formed in the corners of our room. We always woke up hungry. Our meager soups hardly had any flavor and contained little that was nourishing. My stomach rejected this tasteless fare. Even so, Mutti urged me to eat.

During early evening the electricity was cut off for several hours. Candles were not available and so we sat in the dark. When Oma Grunwald visited during the blackouts she entertained us with stories.

Our brother loved to frighten us by stringing objects from the ceiling, which he pulled up and down, wriggling them in front of our faces. One time he used a sad looking doll with no hair or clothes. He was highly pleased when we shrieked with fear.

I don't know how our mother managed to get us through that bitter winter. It must have taken every ounce of her strength. Every day I admired her more.

One day an airmail letter with an American stamp arrived. Who was writing to us? Who knew how to reach us? The four of us jumped around Mutti like a bunch of bunny rabbits, pestering her to open the letter. "Please children, sit at the table and be quiet," she said as she opened the envelope with great ceremony. Several pages of thin airmail paper rustled in the silence as my mother read with deep concentration. I craned my neck, trying to get a glimpse of the unfamiliar writing. Finally, she revealed that the letter was from her American cousins who lived in New York City. We didn't even know that we had relatives in America.

My mother's Aunt Helene, who was my maternal grandmother's sister, immigrated to America with her husband, Heinrich Sebold, in the late 1800's. They settled first in Chicago and later moved to New York. They had five children, but only two daughters survived, Alice and Olga. Before World War II they often came to Breslau during summer vacations. Alice was a graduate of Hunter College and taught German at the High School of Commerce in Manhattan, while Olga taught grade school somewhere in the Bronx. They found us through the Red Cross.

My mother wrote to her cousins, giving them details about our current situation. She told them of empty store shelves and how women and children queued up in long lines when deliveries arrived. She mentioned that winter was especially difficult because of the lack of fuel and warm clothing. Mutti also wrote that we had no news of her mother, their aunt Ottilie, who had left the train in Gleiwitz when we fled Breslau.

Many letters were written and received. Because of their age, we children addressed Cousin Alice and Olga as Tante (aunt). My mother took our measurements and told them how old we were. She traced our feet on tissue paper and let them know that food and all items of clothing would greatly lighten our burden.

One day we received notice that a package was waiting for us at the Post Office. Could it be from America? Peter volunteered to fetch it, but in the end we all went. The Postmaster inspected the large box, making sure it contained only items permitted by the East German government. The package passed inspection and we took turns helping my mother cart the rather heavy load to our humble quarters. It felt like an early Christmas when we spread the contents of the package on the table. There was peanut butter, Spam, chocolate, Vienna Sausages, sardines, and a pound of coffee beans. A red sweater, warm corduroy pants, a light wool blanket and a jacket for my brother were welcomed with joyous shouts. Coffee was not available in East Germany. Although Mutti would have loved to brew a cup, she divided the coffee beans into four packets which she later traded for food.

The packages began to arrive with regularity. We learned that Alice and Olga enlisted the help of their friends and students to collect items of clothing. Olga knew how to sew and the following summer she made colorful cotton dresses for us girls. We looked like butterflies in an otherwise drab landscape.

In my mind's eye I can still see the packages sewn into pillow cases and addressed with thick, black magic marker. They traveled a long way by boat and land, and this assured their safe arrival.

There is no doubt that our American aunts helped us to survive the difficult after-war years. And they brought joy to us girls when they sent coloring books and crayons. One package even contained paper cut-out dolls, providing endless hours of entertainment.

Finally, spring arrived and with it warmer weather and days with more light. A small fenced garden connected to the property. On sunny days the owner's tubercular wife rested there in a chaise lounge covered with warm blankets. Her coughing fits marred an otherwise peaceful setting. We were not allowed to go near her for fear of catching this debilitating disease. I kept looking at the poor woman and would have liked to visit with her.

In late spring we managed to acquire a small plot of land about twenty minutes away from our lodgings. Even a purebred city woman could learn to grow carrots, string beans, onions, radishes, and potatoes. We all helped to hoe, weed and water. Our trusty little wagon came in handy for carting tools and a watering can already filled with water. We visited our small plot at least twice a week, pulling weeds and watering when needed. When it was time to harvest, we were so proud of our accomplishments.

Hunger had become a daily visitor and the vegetables we harvested helped to ease the pain of our empty stomachs. Towards the end of that summer we said goodbye to our makeshift quarters when we moved into a house right across from the factory where we first found shelter. There we shared a fenced-in villa with several families. We believed the owner of the factory had once resided there.

The villa, covered completely with lush looking vines, sat on a knoll on a large piece of property. As soon as we opened the heavy wrought iron gate leading to the house, we felt as if we had entered paradise. To the right of the entrance a large lilac bush would delight us with its deep purple blossoms when it bloomed in the coming spring. To the left and right what had once been flower beds were now vegetable gardens. A path fashioned from flagstones led to eight wide steps, which went to the house and the back of the property. There were several fruit trees in the rear, which provided us with pears and plumbs when in season. To our delight, there was even a small gazebo coveted by us children when we needed a quiet spot for reading or day-dreaming.

A rose garden could be seen to the right of the villa. The roses were in full bloom when we moved in. Their vibrant colors and pleasing scent permeated the air. Tiled walkways divided the flower beds. Overlooking these, three tall birch trees provided shade to a bench which became a favorite resting place for our family. Wheat fields and meadows surrounded this large fenced-in piece of property, giving one the feeling of living in the country.

The Wohnungsamt (Housing Office) allotted us two airy rooms on the ground floor with lots of windows, inlaid parquet floors and high ceilings. From the outside hall one entered a large kitchen, a dream come true for Mutti. A flushing toilet took the place of the latrine. A young couple occupied a third room. What once must have acted as a long, narrow coat closet became their kitchen, where they cooked on a hot plate. This space had no door, only a curtain provided some privacy.

Another family lived upstairs. They were displaced persons from Prussia; an elderly farm couple and their daughter whose son, Horst, was Bärbel's age. We coexisted together. They were country folk and did not exactly warm up to my mother and her sophisticated city ways. We spoke High German, which somehow made us seem different.

Our walk to school was now much further—not an ordeal during good weather, but not so pleasant when it rained or snowed. We had no umbrellas or boots; often we sat in class with wet clothes and feet. No wonder I was out sick so often. Years later I came upon two report cards that stated I had been absent for thirty-six days in one school year and the following year for fifty-two days. I don't remember being sick, only that I had a hospital stay because I suffered from headaches and dizzy spells. The attending Doctor told my mother that he could do little for me. What I needed was nourishing food.

One season followed another and life took on some normalcy. The food shortages eased and we no longer stood in long lines. The packages from America continued to arrive, helping us in countless ways.

During the after-war years, we children had to find our own entertainment. As I recall, we had no toys, not even paper or colored pencils for drawing. In good weather we were always outdoors, playing games of hide and seek or ball games in the street. I especially liked playing school. My little sisters and their friends were my students, until they became tired of being bossed.

In summer we walked to the city pool, located way in the country. The pool, nestled below a forested hill, provided us with many hours of entertainment. People spread their towels and blankets on a spacious meadow and soaked up the sun. I learned to swim on school outings, during which we received swimming lessons from our gym teacher. I remember taking my turn being strapped into a harness and then suspended in the water on a long pole. We were encouraged to make the movements of the breaststroke as shown to us on land. It was really quite hilarious. During those carefree times, our hardships were forgotten and time stood still.

In the fall my sister Bärbel and the boy from upstairs started first grade. Uschi, who was only 15 months younger, felt left out, so Mutti got her the traditional Zuckertüte too. There were now four of us walking to school. Peter always forged ahead; Bärbel and Horst walked side by side. They made a cute couple, though I learned later from Bärbel that she considered him a pest.

I met a girl at school who lived only ten minutes away. We became friends and most days walked to school together. Edith had bright red hair and freckles all over her face. She was an only child and her parents were strict. They expected her to do well in school and insisted on many hours of study, allowing little time for play. We often did our homework at her house, which I loved because if was so quiet and peaceful.

The following spring we planted vegetables, this time on the property surrounding the house. In late summer farmers harvested their wheat fields. This was anticipated by the locals, who were allowed to graze the fields for what was left behind. Mutti was, of course, right there to collect our share of the bounty. I went along to help.

It was late in the afternoon when we joined a crowd waiting at the edge of the field. As soon as the farmer gave his O.K. everyone ran like ants, grabbing whatever they could. I was quite taken aback by people's greedy behavior when they pushed and shoved with no consideration for others.

The stubbles on the field scratched my bare legs. Mutti and I wore half aprons with a large pocket at the bottom. Burlap sacks had been left at the edge of the field, and when our aprons were full, we would empty them into the sack. We were thrilled when our sack got full and we later carted it to the local mill. Our bounty yielded two pounds of flour.

Thus, Mutti was able to bake a cake for us. This took place on Saturdays. Because we had no oven, when the cake was ready for baking, I carried it to the local bakery. For a small fee they baked it for us in their large ovens. A little piece of brown craft paper would be pressed into one corner displaying our name. Others had to do the same, and it was fun to ogle the different cakes being carried to and from the bakery. The delicious odor of the cake made me want to snatch a tiny piece, but I was afraid I would be reprimanded.

Later in the fall we joined other locals during the potato harvest. Equipped with small hoes, we dug into the rich dirt. Many potatoes had been left in the ground, and we eagerly gathered them into our burlap sack. They allowed Mutti to make a tasty potato soup and potato pancakes, a favorite repast.

We also raised rabbits to augment the lack of meat in our diet. They were kept in wooden cages by the side of the house. We children were sent to gather dandelions in neighboring fields to add to their diet of carrots and lettuce. We loved the rabbits and none of us wanted to think about the fact that one day they would be killed. I don't remember who did this. Perhaps the upstairs farmer performed the grisly task.

Before winter set in, Muti ordered cords of wood that were stored near the rabbit cages. We had acquired two sawhorses and a large saw with handles on each side. Peter and I were given the task of sawing the wood into small pieces. As so often happened during those years, Peter managed to annoy me by being uncooperative. Smooth back-and-forth strokes were required, but Peter always pulled in the wrong direction, making this chore more difficult. I don't remember who wielded the ax that split the wood into smaller pieces so they could fit into the tile stove.

Peter and I were also sent to the local lumber yard where, for a small fee, we could gather wood shavings. These were used to start the fire. For this chore we were equipped with two large burlap sacks which, when filled, we carted back in our little wagon.

During one of these outings we met a boy Peter knew. His name was Reinhart and he was just a little taller than me. His hair stood up every which way and he wore black-rimmed glasses that made him look like an owl. He offered to help us, as it was much easier if two people held the burlap sack open. So here we were holding the sack while Peter scooped in the shavings. All of a sudden this boy, a stranger to me, leaned over and tried to kiss me. I was utterly appalled! I tried to stay away from Reinhart from then on.

A small house called the Waschküche (laundry room) sat tucked away to the rear of the property. It was well equipped with several round wooden tubs, scrubbing boards and a long wooden handle for lifting laundry from the big kettle, which stood in the center of the room. The Waschküche's many windows made it bright and especially pleasant on sunny days when the rays provided warmth. A signup sheet hung on the wall, where we would reserve the place for a specific day.

As with all chores, I was my mother's helper on laundry day. One time I wanted to try out the scrubbing board, which intrigued me. Mutti showed me how to hold the garments between my hands and go up and down the scrubbing board with my knuckles. Unfortunately, the powdered laundry detergent we used contained some harsh agents. My fingers became infected and I walked around with bandaged hands for days. No more scrubbing boards for me.

One day Mutti received a letter from her sister, who also escaped from Breslau and had settled in a town not far from us. Tante Fee's husband, like my father, was a prisoner of war in Russia. Tante Fee had the good fortune to find a job as cook and housekeeper at a school for boys. Thus, they had enough food. She had located us through the Red Cross. Ready to overlook whatever differences she and my mother may have had in the past, she was anxious to see us.

And so we met with our aunt, Tante Fee, and our cousin, Bodo, who was two years younger than I. Tante Fee had blonde hair. She and my mother were nearly of the same height, but in every other way they were as different as night and day.

We learned that she and my cousin Bodo had been unable to leave Breslau in January of 1945 because Tante Fee's mother-in-law was in the hospital. Sadly, she died. Tante Fee told Mutti about the awful conditions in Breslau during the last months before the Red Army arrived.

Cousin Bodo was a lively, exuberant boy with an infectious laugh. He soon engaged us in wild and noisy games. He loved to pull the straps of the jalousies way into the room and have them pull him back by their sheer force. Being of a cautious nature, I warned him that the straps might break, but this did not deter him from having his fun. From that time on we stayed in close contact with Tante Fee and whenever possible, she and Bodo would visit us. We all looked forward to those occasions because cousin Bodo was so much fun.

In 1947/48 life took an upturn. Food shortages eased and Mutti was able to cook more nourishing and tastier meals. There are a number of events from that time that I still remember.

We heard from our half-brother, Hannsjoachim, who at the end of the war ended up in the British sector in Northern Germany. He was briefly detained in a British prisoner of war camp. After his release, he found lodging with a kind family with many children. There he flourished and was able to continue his studies. Excitement was great when he wrote that he would come for a visit.

Hannsjoachim was now a young man in his early twenties. His outward appearance had not changed much, but the war had robbed him of precious years of his early youth. He was deeply saddened that there had been no news of our maternal grandmother, who had raised him. To our delight Hannsjoachim was armed with a camera. He took a slew of black and white pictures of us. We proudly posed for him underneath the birch trees. These were the first photos anyone had taken of us in years.

In the spring of 1949 my mother received an official-looking letter informing her that our father would be released from Russia. Our joy was overwhelming. Mutti had carried the burden of raising her four children long enough. What a relief it must have been for her to be reunited with her husband, who had been gone for so many years.

My brother Peter badly needed the influence of a male figure in his life. He had always been a little on the wild side and he needed a father. He, more than us girls, was affected by our father's homecoming. My father's mother, our Oma Grunwald, was beginning to fail. No one put a name on what ailed her. But she seemed determined to live until her only son returned from Russia.

Finally in the spring; I don't exactly remember the month or the day of the week, Mutti and I went to Oschatz, a town five miles away, to welcome my father home. We had no idea what time he was to arrive. We waited for many hours at the train station. The stationmaster was a kind man. He invited us into his office when evening came, and when it grew late, he fashioned a bed for me with two chairs. I fell asleep on his coat smelling of tobacco.

The sun was just rising when a train pulled in. How would he look? Would I recognize him? Would I even like him? These thoughts raced through my mind. Feelings of apprehension lodged in my stomach. Then, there he was, my father! I felt very shy as we hugged. My parents clung to each other in a seemingly endless embrace.

No train was scheduled back to Mügeln, so we went on foot. It was a beautiful day, sunny and crisp with many signs of new beginnings. We walked on narrow paths through fields that had been planted with spring crops. My parents talked nonstop. They had so much to share, years of happenings needed to be covered. I listened quietly to the hum of their voices. I don't remember how long it took us to get home.

There was an air of celebration; our family was united at last. We huddled together and listened to the stories Vati had to tell. It took several days before we adjusted to his presence. He was now the authority; there was no doubt about that. We three girls had no difficulty in adhering to our father's discipline, though my brother Peter rebelled for a while. But we were a family again and that brought security. The biggest change was in my mother, who shed the heavy load she had carried for so long. She was able to relax, knowing that whatever happened in the future would be shared with her husband.

It was fortuitous that the young couple occupying the third room on the ground floor had found their own apartment, enabling my parents to have their own bedroom.

Vati told us many stories about how he survived being a prisoner of war in Russia. They were fascinating and we listened intently, though the depth of them was at times way over our heads.

Vati's first year in Russia was difficult. He was in Siberia where the winters were severe. Everyone was sent for hours into the forest to cut down trees. The prisoner's clothes were makeshift, not sufficient to shield them from the severe weather. Frostbite was the norm of the day, and they never had enough to eat. Many of the men were unable to withstand the inhuman conditions and they folded like matchsticks.

Among the prisoners were doctors, lawyers, musicians, plumbers—every occupation was represented. Their combined life experiences allowed them to fashion all sorts of things from almost nothing. Musical instruments were built from scratch and when the musicians performed their first concert, many of the men cried tears of happiness. That must have been a touching experience, as music opens the heart and releases feelings and emotions. Eventually my father was moved to Minsk, a town in White Russia. There he was indoctrinated in the teachings of Communism and he was no longer required to do hard labor.

As a result, Vati quickly found employment with the local labor union under Communist rule. Our life improved in many ways. We had more money and the first item my father purchased was a radio. Vati loved classical music and he would tune in to many symphony concerts. He also loved flowers and plants and soon decorated our sparse living room with them.

The reunion between Oma Grunwald and my father was touching. Soon after his return, she entered the hospital and died of a heart attack on June 1, my father's birthday. This was my first exposure to death. For our funeral attire, Mutti died our skirts black and we wore these with white blouses and black ribbons in our hair.

On the day of the funeral we walked solemnly to the cemetery, where the local pastor conducted a brief service in the cemetery chapel. A few neighbors came to pay their respects. I remember feeling very sad and I know my father was deeply touched by the loss of his mother. But the next day life went on as always. I sat in class overcome with grief; tears flowed down my face. A male teacher came to ask me what was wrong. When I told him that my grandmother had died he just shrugged his shoulders and told me to stop crying.

That same summer a little kitten found its way to our doorstep. She was the cutest ball of fur, with gray/black and white markings. We fell in love with her and named her Muschi. In those days cat food was not sold in stores and pets shared the family fare. We fed her dishes of milk and table scraps. Muschi became an important part of our family. We never tired of playing with her. She often disappeared for hours, roaming the neighborhood.

Weeks after we adopted her, she returned home early one evening completely covered in black tar. Muschi had been across the street to the factory where she must have fallen into a pool of tar. She looked pitiful and bedraggled, and meowed something awful. My parents tried to bathe her, but the tar would not come off. We all hovered around her to give her comfort. Eventually, our parents sent us to bed. They kept watch over Muschi all night, but by morning she had died. All of us were heartbroken and my sisters and I cried our eyes out.

Postcard of Mügeln

Mutti with Peter, Bärbel, Uschi, and me
in our American finery

Bärbel's first day of school with
Zuckertüte, (Uschi on left)

Tante Fee and cousin Bodo

Return to Dresden

In the spring of 1950, my father received an offer for an important position in Dresden. East Germany had lost many of its influential and artistic people when they fled to the West. Russia felt that Culture and Art were important and much effort was expended to re-establish Dresden as a cultural city. My father's excellent people skills and his deep interest in the arts made him the perfect candidate to head the labor unions responsible for Art and Culture.

Vati left for Dresden where he located a furnished apartment on the Käte Kollwitz-Ufer, so named in 1945 after a German painter, printmaker and sculptor whose work offered a searing account of the human condition. She died in May of 1945. The Käte Kollwiotz-Ufer curved for miles along the Elbe River, which was badly polluted.

Dresden had been northern Germany's cultural center – a city filled with museums and historic buildings. Before World War II it was called "the Florence on the Elbe" and considered one of the world's most beautiful cities owing to its architecture and art treasures. However, in the 1950's, because Russia put their effort into rebuilding destroyed cities in Russia rather than rebuilding eastern Germany, much of the city center remained rubble. So when we arrived in Dresden I did not see any of the city's beauty.

The many burned-out buildings were a constant reminder of the horrific air raid which destroyed so much of the city in February of 1945. On some streets the rubble had not even been cleared away. It felt like a dark cloud was hovering above, a feeling that never left me during our less than a year's stay.

Because Dresden was the capital of Saxony, there was more evidence of the Russian occupation. Posters depicting Stalin, Lenin and other Communist leaders were displayed all over the city, as well as party slogans, which were the only color in evidence among the drab buildings.

I was apprehensive about entering a new school, partly because I was feeling uncomfortable with the changes taking place in my body. It seemed like my breasts were growing with incredible speed. I often walked with my arms crossed over my chest in an attempt to cover these bulges. There was no talk about getting me a bra. I also got my first period during a gym class, which frightened me until Mutti explained what I had to look forward to on a monthly basis. She appeared to be uneasy when we talked and so I asked few questions.

Going to a new school was traumatic. I was extremely shy, wanting to disappear into my skin. I did make one friend, a girl who was motherless. I was attracted to her because she, too, was a refugee from the east. Irmgard had a large birthmark on one side of her face, which made her stand out. She looked after two younger brothers and took care of all household chores. I often spent time at her apartment, where we were unsupervised. Though our friendship was short-lived, I was grateful for the times we shared.

In school we were encouraged to join The Young Pioneers, a Communist youth organization. We met once a week after school and wore white blouses and red kerchiefs around our neck. We learned all about the history of Communism and its leaders. We had to march in parades when Communist holidays and events were celebrated. The parades ended in a huge square, where we listened to long, boring speeches by important Communist leaders, who warned us about capitalism and its bad influence on the world.

Under the German educational system, only eight years of school were required. After graduation most students went on to study a trade. Those who wanted to go on to higher education had to be approved by the government. Preference was given to the children of working class people; the sons and daughters of doctors, lawyers and other academics were put on the bottom of the list. It helped if your parents were members of the Communist Party. Because my father was working for the government, I was assured a spot in the Upper School for the following year. I dreamed of becoming a teacher.

Life and its activities flowed on an even keel for a time. One day my father arrived home with a boxer puppy, a gift from a coworker. Vati loved animals and he was thrilled with this new addition to our family. We named him Tarzan. The name turned out to be appropriate, as he was wild and untamable. He behaved well for my father, but during Vati's absence, it was difficult to keep Tarzan contained.

I dreaded taking Tarzan for his walk. A garbage dump not far from the river Elbe was an attraction for him, and he strained to be free to frolic among the enticing smells. I recall one incident when he pulled me so hard that I fell and was dragged for several feet before I let go of his leash. I was wearing a new dress, fashioned from a light wool plaid blanket we had received from America. A huge triangle was torn into the skirt portion. I was heartbroken. It took the whole family to catch our vagrant dog, but I eventually forgave Tarzan. After all, he was so lovable and affectionate.

While we were living in Dresden, letters went back and forth from our house to New York City and packages continued to arrive, though their frequency had lessened. We were still on rationing cards, even for clothing, and everything we received was put to good use. Mutti was well dressed when she and Vati went to the Opera, concerts, ballets and other performances several times a week. Vati wore colorful American ties that eventually got him into trouble with the Communists.

That summer my American aunts took their first trip to Europe since before World War II. They invited my mother and Tante Fee to meet them in West Berlin. Mutti and my two sisters went. To this day, I don't know why I could not have been a part of this trip. I imagine that someone had to stay back and take care of my father and brother.

Mutti and my sisters returned with exciting accounts about their adventures in West Berlin. They were treated to delicious meals, and they had fun seeing the sights. Mutti welcomed this opportunity to thank her cousins in person for all they were doing for us. I was delighted that they still wanted me to come for a visit to New York. Sadly, the East German government forbade foreign travel.

One fine spring day in 1951, Mutti took Peter and me aside and told us that we had to flee East Germany. Our father had been interrogated by the secret police on two occasions. He feared that this was only the beginning of harassment and could lead to eventual imprisonment. Vati was already in West Berlin, my mother said, and Peter and I were to follow the next day. Mutti was very serious. There were to be no goodbyes. She impressed on us to not tell a soul, as this could jeopardize our escape.

Mutti wrote a letter giving us permission to visit an imaginary aunt for a week's vacation in East Berlin. This was before the wall was up separating the east and west parts of the city. We packed a small suitcase with everything we would need for such a short trip. Once again, we would be leaving everything else behind.

For me it was a déjà vu experience, reminiscent of our departure from Breslau in 1945. I trembled on the inside, fearful of what would await us in Berlin, and was sad that I could not say goodbye to my friend. Vati had already made arrangements for Tarzan, who could not accompany us. Mutti assured us that she would follow with my two sisters in just a few days.

Escape to West Berlin

Berlin was the capital of Germany. During World War II it was virtually destroyed by bombing, artillery, and ferocious street-to-street fighting. After the war, Germany was split into four occupied zones; Berlin, which ended up in East Germany under Russian occupation, would also have an American, British, and French sector. Before the erection of the Berlin Wall in August of 1961, it was relatively easy to slip into West Berlin. Thousands applied for asylum for political reasons, as well as those who simply desired to live in the more prosperous West.

The train sped towards Berlin. Most of the compartments were crowded, but Peter and I were able to get two window seats. At age fourteen, such things as having a window seat and going on a trip can be terribly exciting. For just a moment I forgot the real purpose of this train ride. But that did not last long. We were fleeing from Communist Germany to West Berlin. In those days it was still relatively easy to get across the border. Once in Berlin, we could board the S-Bahn (subway) and ride into West Berlin.

The trains were spot-ckecked, of course, and if you happened to be on the black list, it would mean prison or labor camp. As I said, my brother and I were pretending that we were going to visit an aunt in East Berlin; that was the story we would tell if someone stopped us. My brother was my chaperone, and being sixteen, he was ever so confident; it was hard to tell what his true feelings were.

I had difficulty breathing. I was afraid and worried that everyone could see it. Looking out of the window no longer was of interest and I began to scrutinize fellow passengers to see if they might know what we were up to. I don't recall their faces. They must have been friendly people, but their visages remain as grimaces in my memory.

Shortly before we reached Berlin two Vopos (slang for East German policemen) entered our compartment. I could feel tears coming to my eyes. My brother gave me a push. It was just enough to distract me for a few minutes as my fright changed into anger at my bossy, older brother.

The Vopos opened our suitcase and read the letter my mother had written, giving her permission for this trip. Peter was so sure of himself. He was excellent in sports and had won many competitions, and he was now wearing every medal he had ever received. He also wore a lapel pin identifying him as a young Communist. This made him look like a reliable East German youth. I admired his gall as he joked with the police. Finally it was all over and I could relax.

Every German has his own vision of Berlin, and as we approached my anticipation of seeing this capital grew. When we finally arrived in East Berlin I was disappointed. It looked as drab as Dresden. Bombed-out buildings were visible everywhere and people did not look cosmopolitan at all.

We quickly found the entrance to the S-Bahn. I had my brother count out how many East German stops there would be to the West Zone of Berlin. At each stop my heart beat loudly and I was sure everyone could hear it. As in the train, police appeared on the scene and checked identifications at random. And then it happened!

Across from us sat a middle-aged couple. He wore simple work clothes and his companion an inexpensive, colorless dress. A huge shopping bag like most Germans use when they do their daily errands, sat on the floor. The policemen stopped in front of them and asked for their papers. They glanced at a list and looked at each other and nodded. The unfortunate couple was asked to get off the train at the next stop. The woman was shaking with fright and the man tried to protest, but I guess there was little anyone could do. People in the car had very sympathetic looks on their faces, but no one dared to help.

I watched in horror and imagined that we would be next. Luckily, the next stop was in the West sector and we hurried from the train. My brother told me that we were safe. I wanted to cry, but Peter would have called me some unflattering names, so I swallowed a few times and tried to breathe in the air of freedom.

In East Germany we were told how police used their clubs to beat people in the West and how America was using West Germany to their advantage. We were told that Russia was our best friend and we, the young, were going to grow up into Communists and defend the freedom of the world. So my feelings were divided and I was not sure what to expect.

My father was waiting for us on the platform of the station. I don't know how long he had waited. We embraced and said little. I know he was relieved to see us.

We emerged from the station and I stood still, looking in wonder at the scene that opened in front of my eyes. I was not familiar with billboard advertisements and there were so many. In the East Zone the only advertisements were slogans and pictures of Communist statesmen. Here I felt vibrant life embracing all of me. A sea of color brought things to one's attention.

And then there were the people; so beautifully dressed. The stores displayed wares in their windows that I had not seen before. In the East, as I said, we were still on rationing cards and the shelves in the stores were often bare.

We stopped at the first vegetable stand. Peter and I stared at the abundance of fruit and vegetables. There were fruits we had not seen before, much less tasted. Oranges, bananas, pineapples! I know my father didn't have much money, but he reached into his pocket and bought us each a banana. I did not even know how to peel it and so Vati did it for me. I could hardly wait to take a bite as my father watched with anticipation. My brother looked at me and I looked at him and we grinned. We did not think much of that mealy, mushy taste, and to my father's disappointment, we both agreed that bananas were not our cup of tea. Later on we got to taste oranges and those we could have munched ten at a time.

My father had been staying with a cousin whom we had not

met. She lived in a beautiful apartment with 10-foot ceilings and cozy rooms. Everything was tastefully furnished with antiques and soft, comfortable chairs and couches that hugged one's body. She asked us to call her Tante Else and made us feel welcome.

Two days later, my mother with my two younger sisters arrived. At the time, I did not fully understand what dangers we had all faced and it didn't occur to me that my mother and sisters might not make it. My father paced like a caged animal, his face distorted with worry. Train after subway train arrived and left. Finally, the doors of a train opened and there they were. We were a family again and that was all that counted for the moment.

We needed to register as refugees and we children tagged along to the refugee receiving station. We had been used to long queues in the East, so the throngs of people did not perturb us. There was a great deal of red tape, forms to fill out and there were official looking people with whom my parents had to speak. We amused ourselves by finding other kids and started a discussion about our new lives and hopes for the future. Everyone had an interesting story to tell on how he or she escaped and with the danger now gone, these stories became adventures.

Some of the girls told us that they couldn't bring a suitcase and instead, they were wearing many layers of clothes. I had wondered why so many of them looked overweight. They were smart enough to put on three changes of underwear, extra skirts, blouses and dresses. We formed quick friendships, only to be disappointed when we were assigned to different shelters.

We boarded a streetcar to take us to our destination. Once we began moving, I felt violently sick and begged to be let off. I must have been going through hormonal changes. Motion sickness stayed with me for the next two years. My mother sympathized with me, but encouraged me to hold on a little longer.

We arrived in a lovely section of Berlin, called Wilmersdorf. Located in the British sector in a primarily residential area, the streets were quiet and it was difficult to tell if the big mansions were occupied at all. Not far away the Grunewald forest stretched for miles. We later discovered a large lake there, where in good weather we spent much of our time.

The Red Cross Shelter was not far away from Hohenzollerndam, a main junction, and we walked to the address that had been given to us. All the rumors I had heard during the day about the various shelters were going through my mind. I was trying to picture what ours would be like. When we arrived we faced a huge, bare white house with a high fence around it. A few trees grew in the garden, but the grounds were barren and where once grass and flowers had grown, dirty sand had taken over. A large red cross at the front gate indicated that this facility was being run by the Red Cross. I still remember the address: Kronenbergstrasse 20. We had to ring a bell to gain entrance.

A middle-aged man ushered us in and told us to wait in the hall. He went to fetch the Red Cross nurse who was in charge. A tall, stern woman came down the wide staircase that led to the upper floor. She wore wire-rimmed glasses and her eyes were cold. She led the way to her office, which was located upstairs.

I saw several large rooms on the main floor. At one time these were probably the dining room, a ballroom and a winter garden. The hall was wood paneled and its once beautiful parquet floors were now without luster. They had been scrubbed with water and soap and though they looked clean, there was nothing pretty about them.

The upstairs had many rooms. Whoever was assigned to one of them was called lucky. They were the elite, and I later found out that the people downstairs did not like the people who lived upstairs.

Nurse Erika had a large office. Formerly a library, the room was completely wood paneled and two walls had floor to ceiling bookshelves. She explained about life at this facility. She mentioned that this was a transient camp where people arrived and departed on a daily basis. There were lots of rules to follow: Cleaning schedules, meal schedules, bathing schedules – all run by the clock. We were assigned to the infirmary on our first night. A room would become available the next day, when we could settle into our temporary home.

We children had stood quietly while all the talking and seemingly friendly exchanges went on. Nurse Erika gave us a benevolent look from time to time and told us that we would have lots of fun. We did not know what fun she was referring to but smiled back. We were tired and the tension and excitement of the last few days had begun to take its toll.

The infirmary was the prettiest room in the house. I liked it immediately and wished we could stay there. It was large, with lots of windows, adorned with white lace curtains. There was not much to do but get acquainted with our surroundings. Dinner would be served in less than an hour. I felt shy and did not want to be looked over by all the people I had noticed staring at us upon our arrival. Only later did I find out what fun it was to speculate on new arrivals when we summed them up in those first few moments.

On our first evening I had no idea how complex life would be in this small camp. How much I would have to watch my step in dealing with the different people and how important it was to be on good terms with everyone. Privacy was what everyone craved, so difficult to attain under these circumstances.

Upstairs there was a washroom with cold-running water and two toilets with a sink. Downstairs there were two dormitory style rooms that I glimpsed as we walked into the dining room. There were so many beds and I could not imagine going to sleep with all the noise and lights burning. The beds were bunks and some were totally covered with blankets on both sides. That is where women undressed and some people slept that way, too. How did they breathe? There were bathroom facilities also on the lower level.

The dining room was a long, narrow room furnished with wooden tables and benches. People sat playing cards, writing letters, and reading. Some just stared blankly into space. No one knew who had occupied this huge mansion, which must have been beautiful in its day.

The Winter Garden was used as a playroom, the only place where children could be noisy. From there a few steps led into the garden, which was not much more than trodden down dirt. Several large trees provided some shade on hot days and the few scraggly looking bushes along the fence had not been cared for in a long time. Nevertheless, here children could throw a ball, play hopscotch or jump rope. Things could get quite depressing in the house, and it seemed that children were always escaping to it when things got steamy inside.

My brother Peter, who was sixteen, was sent to a group home for young boys between the ages of sixteen and twenty-one. They were kept busy re-foresting the Grunewald (a nearby forest) which had been badly depleted during World War II, when firewood was in short supply. This was probably for the best, as our living conditions at the time had nothing to offer a young strapping teenager. As it turned out, he eventually reached West Germany, where he worked on a farm for one year. He later applied to a police academy and became a policeman.

That night I tossed in my bed. The events of the last few days were running wild in my mind. And then my thoughts went back to the other time when we had left all our belongings behind and had departed from Breslau with just a small suitcase. My last thoughts were of my classmates and what they must have thought when I no longer showed up in school.

The room that was to be ours for the next year was no larger than 9 x 12 feet. It was furnished with four bunk beds, a small table with three chairs and a washbasin with running cold water. There were two windows that provided light. The beds were arranged in two groups with an aisle between them. When everyone was present it was impossible to walk around and so we sat on the beds. I felt lucky to get an upper bunk.

We shared the room with a young couple who occupied two of the lower beds. They had come from Czechoslovakia. Their journey to West Berlin had been fraught with much danger. They were waiting for papers that would get them to Canada where they had relatives.

There were so many things to observe. At lunchtime, we were served a warm meal in the large dining room. The food was cooked at another facility and brought by truck by two men who carried the heavy kettles to the basement kitchen. Here, Sister Elisabeth ruled with an iron hand. She was a tiny woman and one had to wonder how she managed to be in charge of feeding close to sixty people. She enlisted the help of several women each day. The food was bland, but we ate it, glad to have a meal. I dreaded Friday, when a concoction of fish cooked in a white mealy sauce was offered. The smell of it could make one sick. It made me feel nauseous and I satisfied myself with just the boiled potatoes that were served with the fish stew.

Mr. and Mrs. Ritter sat at our table. He was a retired German officer who had been on active duty during World War II. Tall and slender, he spent much time caring for his now graying mustache. His clothes were immaculate. During his eloquent talks about his heroism during the war, he would lovingly stroke his mustache, always brushing it in both directions. They had come from Leipzig where Mr. Ritter was harassed by the East German government because of his refusal to join the Communist party. They had been in this Red Cross shelter for two months, and Mr. Ritter never tired of comparing this experience to life in the army. He suggested all sorts of strict rules, and he would have loved to blow a bugle so we could stand for reveille. Fortunately, no one paid much attention to him. The Ritters were childless, which accounted for the little patience they had with children.

In the next few weeks my parents found themselves busy meeting with different committees that handled the cases of East German refugees. We had been granted temporary asylum, but so far were not recognized and accepted to make grade "A". The regulations read as follows: "To be recognized and granted West German citizenship, the life of the person who applied for such rights, needed to have been endangered." What criteria were used to determine this was a mystery. Some people were easily accepted and others were rejected. They preferred if you had been in prison or escaped through the back door, while the police knocked on your front door.

Whenever my mother was absent I took over her duties. She had been assigned to clean the washrooms and toilets on our floor. Old Mrs. Tauber was my assistant, or I was hers. She came to fetch me around nine every morning. I immediately took an aversion to her. She was not much taller than me, but wide as a barrel. Her hair was greasy and she had twisted it together in the back, until she achieved the effect of a little pig's tail hanging over her broad shoulders. She was missing two front teeth, and when she smiled in her false, sweet way, I was thinking of the witch in the story of Hänsel and Gretel.

Mrs. Tauber told me that she was much too old to clean the toilets and that she would prefer if I took over that chore. I was young and could surely clean them in no time. I had been taught to respect my elders and felt that I had no choice but to agree to this arrangement. I fetched a pail and mop and imagined that I was going into battle. I was trying hard to make a joke out of the whole thing, but it was difficult not to get sick to my stomach. I had cleaned bathrooms before, but cleaning the mess twenty people made during the course of a day was hard to take.

Everyone washed themselves at two sinks with a large mirror behind. There also were two toilet stalls. The floor was often swimming with water, paper from razor blades; loose hair of all colors, with shaving cream as decoration. I wasted little time and attacked my job with a vengeance. I felt anger, the only weapon I could use to get through the next half-hour. Later on my pride took over and I felt I could face almost anything.

More and more I was experiencing peculiar mood swings. My mother said it was all part of growing up, but to me it was more than that. I tried to make sense of my predicament. How long would we have to be here? Who would clothe us when fall came? What was my role, and how would I get along with the many different people? What about schooling? My mind was unable to form clear thoughts on any of these questions. I desperately tried to find my way; to find something I could grasp, something that would give meaning to all of this. I was constantly looking for work, the urge to be busy always present. Books made me sad; I was unable to concentrate.

Nurse Erika must have grown tired of me when I pestered her to give me something to do. She let me wax all the furniture in her office, clean her small apartment, and help her sort piles of donated clothing that arrived every week. And still I was not satisfied. One day she asked me to gather all the children in the Winter Garden, the large room with the red tile floor and no furniture. I had been so busy with my own problems that it did not occur to me to help the children. When they came to the Winter Garden I went through my repertoire of stories, games and songs. It was fun. They were adorable, all eyes and ears. I loved them and they in turn loved me. Their mothers and all the residents were also delighted and I was called the Kinder Tante (children's aunt) from then on. No day passed when we did not get together and I am grateful to those children for giving meaning to my uprooted life.

To the frustrating annoyance of the grownups, and to our delight and fun, Saturday was set aside as universal bathing day. The laborious preparations that went into something normally so simple were enormous. The bodily cleansing took place in what once must have been a washroom and tool shed. The small annex to the house had a stone floor and many windows which were covered with torn black shades, leftover from the blackout days during the war. There was nothing cozy about it. A kettle of enormous proportions stood in one corner and tin tubs in various sizes and shapes were neatly placed in another. A few rough-hewn benches completed this décor.

The kettle was resting on bricks, which had an opening to make a fire. During the week the women were boiling their laundry in it, and used the tubs for washing our few garments. Since there were so many families, each was allowed just one hour for bathing every second week. Our turn came one Saturday and I felt like we were going on a big excursion. Soap, towels and a clean change of clothes were carried to the bathing parlor.

We stood in front of the closed door, patiently waiting for the Walter family to clear out. They were evidently not quite ready because Mrs. Walter kept calling out that we should please allow them a few more minutes. Finally the door swung open as they filed out, noticeably cleaner than when they had gone in. The water in the kettle was not hot and we had to be satisfied with lukewarm water. My two sisters and I shared the same bath water since our parents bathed after us, and we could only change the water once. I was just undressing when I noticed a few interested eyes peeking into a window. I refused to climb into the tub until my mother chased the children away and she covered up some of the holes in the shades. It was not the best bath, but it felt so good to be in warm water and we scrubbed ourselves from head to toe in the most privacy we had experienced in a long time. During the next year we often made the trip to the bathhouse and we got into small fights about whose fault it was when the water did not get hot enough.

Weeks passed and my father had still not been recognized as an official refugee. Our hopes of getting to the West Zone of Germany grew dimmer with each passing day. It was decided that we children should attend school. My sisters were enrolled in grade school and I went to a Gymnasium (high school). I was not far behind in my subjects, except for English. Schools in East Germany taught Russian only, which I had studied for three years. Since the students had already had English for five years, there was no way I could catch up.

I felt awkward and out of place. I wore second hand clothes and shoes that did not fit well. My heels were often blistered and covered with Band Aids. My classmates were kind and accepted me; my discomfort was of my own making. There were times when I had difficulty concentrating because I was always thinking about our status as refugees. I seldom participated in school outings because of a lack of money.

When a willowy, blonde girl befriended me I wondered what prompted her to take me under her wing. Her name was Inge. She was a few inches taller than me and very attractive. Her charming smile and welcoming demeanor endeared her to many. She belonged to a youth group, the Nature Lovers, and introduced me to their activities. During their weekly meetings I enjoyed being with young people my own age. That summer my sisters and I met Inge and others at the Grunewald Lake for sunbathing and swimming, times when we could forget our homeless status. It always amused me that the lake was called Grunewald and our last name was Grunwald.

My father had been in contact with several of his comrades from his years in Russia, who lived in West Germany. One of them found him a job in a factory in Mohnheim, a small town in the Rhineland. Though the job was not in his line of work, he accepted it as a way to get his family to West Germany.

Before Vati's departure we celebrated Christmas and New Year's Eve at Tante Else's apartment. We dressed in our finest clothes, grateful to have this opportunity to enjoy a delicious meal in the atmosphere of a private home.

By now Tante Else's apartment had become a familiar haven for me. Sensitive to the feelings of a teenager, Tante Else invited me on many occasions to have dinner and spend the night. I loved escaping from the Red Cross Shelter and reveled in the peaceful atmosphere of Tante Else's apartment. She allowed me to browse her library and listen to music on her radio. Sadly, these visits stopped when we were transferred to another camp the following year. The distance was simply too far.

After Vati departed for West Germany we were once again without our father. At the time we did not know that it would be over a year before we would see him again. He wrote to us often and told us of his lonely and difficult life. He had rented a tiny attic room and was cooking his meals on an electric hotplate. We missed him very much, just as he missed us.

The monotony of shelter life continued. Some families departed for the West Zone and new ones arrived. Their stories had much in common and yet, each family had its individual cross to bear. In time unrest settled in, especially among those who had been in the shelter for a long time. A few disgruntled people formed a committee to protest the leadership and complain about the food. Management viewed this as a type of mutiny and the shelter was dissolved.

We packed our things and moved to another part of Berlin, this time far away from the center of the city. This was a refugee camp and it was located in Buckow, close to the Havel River. Across from the river was East Berlin. People were always on edge, as border crossings by East German police had been reported.

Our life changed drastically at the camp. It had a dismal look about it. Grey barrack-type buildings spread over a wide area with not a tree or anything green in sight. Unpaved roads turned into mud when it rained. There was one blessing; we no longer had to share a room with others. Mutti tried to make our place cozy with the little we had. But most difficult for me—my schooling ended, as there was no school close by. My sisters fared better; they were enrolled in a grade school a distance away.

Once again I was given the opportunity to gather little children in a small room, which gave meaning to my boring and empty days. Here I honed my skills in inventing games, telling stories and added to my repertoire of children's songs. I begged for and obtained books for young children, which provided pleasure for the little ones and taught me to read aloud in a dramatic way.

One day a kind lady who was visiting our camp offered me a job. She asked if I would be interested in cleaning her home on a weekly basis. I jumped at the chance to earn a little money and to get away from camp. Though I did not want to spend my life cleaning houses, I embraced my job with enthusiasm. I was allowed to play the radio; how wonderful it was to hear music again. One time strains of a beautiful melody caught my attention. It went straight to my heart and I began to dance. I felt such a longing. Could one be sad and happy at the same time? Later, I learned that the music was from the ballet "Romeo and Juliet".

With my first earnings I went to see a movie. I could find no one who wanted to go with me and walked the two miles by myself. "For Whom the Bell Tolls" was playing, a story based on Ernest Hemingway's novel. Ingrid Bergman and Gary Cooper starred in it. As soon as the lights went out I forgot everything around me. My whole being lived the unfolding story flashing on the small movie screen. When it was over I had trouble returning to reality. I could not stop crying, and walked back to the camp with tears streaming down my face. All the hurts as well as the joys of the whole world seemed to be resting on my shoulders. There was no one to share this with, and that made me sad. In those days we did not talk about our feelings and I'm not even sure if I would have been able to find the right words to express them.

Time at the new camp passed slowly. We still did not know when we would be sent to West Germany. Our birthdays came and went without much celebration; I would turn sixteen on my next one. The weather was bleak, which did not help to improve our moods. The little stove in our small room could not keep us warm and we were always cold. Layers of clothes were worn to bed. For meals, we trudged wearily to the dining barrack, eating only to stay alive, since nothing tasted good.

One night an alarm sounded. We were told that the Russians planned to take over our camp. We were terrified. It did not happen, but the false rumor took hold of my imagination and I had frequent dreams about being taken prisoner by the Russians.

Where there is darkness there must also be light, for one can't exist without the other. Spring finally announced itself with singing birds, the sun began to warm our cold bones, and we received the news that we were going to West Germany. Our current camp was overflowing with refugees and room had to be made for new arrivals. My mother was so happy. Throughout all this time she had been strong, always fighting for our survival, just as she had done in 1945. I loved and admired her so.

We left Berlin from the Tempelhof airport, our first flight experience. The plane was small, powered by propellers. We settled in our seats, full of excitement. What a wonder it was to lift up into the air and fly among the clouds. Unfortunately, soon after take-off we hit some air pockets. The plane would drop fifty feet. This happened a number of times, making some people sick. The paper sacks provided in the seat pockets came in handy when the woman sitting next to me vomited.

In School in Berlin – front row white blouse

Children in front of Red Cross Shelter

My friend Inge (second from left) with my family at
Tante Else's in Berlin

An overnight at Tante Else's

West Germany at Last

I don't remember to which airport we flew. It might have been Munich because we were bused to a holding camp somewhere in Bavaria. The camp was located on a hill, with a breathtaking view. We could see mountains and a tiny town nestled in the valley. We only stayed there for a few days. Our next stop was the small town of Langenfeld, located in the Rhineland, not far from Cologne and Düsseldorf.

There we settled into a large room above a restaurant that once served as a party room. Dividers had been erected and each 8-ft. cubicle was assigned to a family. As there was no ceiling, one could hear everything and lights shone into the night. By now I had learned to sleep with my arms covering my ears and face to shut out noise and light.

We were a small group of families, all waiting for permanent housing assignments. We cooked our meals on hot plates that had been set up in one corner. I believe we did our own shopping with money allotted to us by the government. There was a backyard with several large fruit trees, providing entertainment for boys who climbed into their branches. On nice days we ate outside on picnic tables.

My father was not far away; so on the very first Sunday we walked to Mohnheim, a forty minute hike. Vati was waiting for us and we could not get enough of his embraces and kisses. He looked haggard; the work in the factory had put a strain on his health. We barely fit into his tiny attic room, but no one cared. We were together. These visits became a ritual and we always made Eierkuchen (crepes), which we ate sprinkled with sugar or applesauce. My sister, Bärbel, remembers that our parents urged us to go for a walk as soon as the dishes had been washed. I chuckle now, as it did not occur to me then what they had in mind.

Our goal was to receive housing that would accommodate our family and a desk job for my father. No one knew how long this would take. My sisters were enrolled in school, thrilled to make friends and continue their learning. My situation, however, was quite different. I had missed so much schooling that it was felt I would not be able to catch up. One day my father came upon an advertisement in the newspaper, placed by a dentist who was looking to train a young woman as a dental assistant. My parents urged me to apply. I didn't like dentists because of an unfortunate childhood experience, but I felt I had little choice since no other options presented themselves. I made an appointment for an interview.

Dr. Schultke was middle aged, on the short and chubby side, with a dour demeanor. I don't know why he thought I might be right for the position, but he left message with the restaurant downstairs to say that I could begin the training. I was so nervous and scared. Deep down I didn't feel confident that this was the right job for me. Nevertheless, we purchased a white cotton coat that I was to wear over my street clothes.

I began work on a Monday when I was given a tour and instructions regarding my duties. I was to set up the instruments before each patient arrived, stand next to the chair when the dentist worked on patients, and hand him instruments as instructed. I was shown how to sterilize everything when the procedure was complete. One day a week I attended a trade school where theory was taught. I liked that a lot better than working in the dentist's office.

Summer came to an end. Life was as normal as it could be living under makeshift conditions. Our weekly visits with our father were celebrated. In spite of the narrowness of his quarters, we were able to be together as a family and share all the events of the week.

Sometime in August a letter arrived from my American aunts. My mother had stayed in contact with them, keeping them informed of each new address. It was not until Mutti had shared the letter with my father that I learned of its content. My aunts had invited me to spend time with them in New York. They had already applied for a Visitor's Visa and had looked into booking a passage on a ship for some time in late September.

I was speechless. Did I want to go? Did I want to give up my dental training? The pros and cons flew back and forth as the subject was heatedly discussed. I don't think my parents wanted me to go to New York, but by the same token, they realized what an extraordinary opportunity was being offered to me. Ultimately the decision was mine.

How could I not want to go to New York? America, the land where streets were paved with gold, beckoned. I dreaded to tell Dr. Schultke about my plan. He was quite put out and let me know how he had invested time in training me and was now faced with starting all over. I in turn was not in the least bit sorry to leave, especially since he once "mortally" wounded me by complaining about my smelly feet. The shoes I wore were not made of leather and did not allow for my feet to breathe.

Fall arrived in splendor; leaves slowly turned into shades of gold and red. Chestnut trees dropped their fruit and my sisters and their friends collected as many as they could, cracking them open and admiring the shiny brown nuts that emerged. They fashioned many things from the chestnuts, using little sticks and toothpicks when we could get them. All sorts of animals came into being and soon there was a wonderful collection; providing hours of entertainment.

Finally, in late September 1953, I found myself on a ship on my way to America. Little did I know how this would change my life.

New York - a New Vision

My aunts had booked a passage on a small Italian ship that was to leave from Bremerhaven on September 25. My mother had a cousin who lived in Bremen and she contacted him to see if he would meet my train, keep me overnight and deliver me to the ship. When we lived in Breslau I had never heard of any relatives, and now they seemed to appear from nowhere.

Mutti and I went to Cologne, where we met my half-brother, Hannsjoachim. He was living not far away and came to give me a proper send-off. I had seen little of him since the war and was surprised to meet a young man of 28 who had completed his studies and was now employed in preparing upcoming teachers for their exams. We spent the night in an inexpensive Pension and I remember that we went to see a movie, "The Third Man," a 1949 British thriller. It was set in post-war Vienna. To this day I am transported to that evening whenever I hear the theme music from that film. The next day my mother and brother saw to it that I boarded the right train. I don't think I cried, but I certainly felt like it. I waved goodbye as the train picked up speed. Then I was alone, so very alone.

I recognized Onkel Vincent and his wife Meta from my mother's description. I was relieved when they met my train on the platform of the Bremen railroad station. We took a streetcar to their small apartment. They made me feel welcome. Tante Meta was short, bowlegged and not very pretty, but her kindness soon made me forget her looks. Onkel Vinzent had a wonderful laugh and he was very good looking. During supper he told me that his mother and my grandmother were sisters, and that he had spent most of his childhood in Upper Silesia. The night I spent on their living room couch was restless.

The next day we departed for Bremerhaven, a large port city. Many ships lay anchored in the harbor. When I spotted the Neptunia, I got cold feet. It was not very large, but to me it looked like a giant. Onkel Vinzent sensed my unease. He gave me a warm hug and assured me that all would be well. One last wave to my hosts and it was time to walk up the gangplank.

A sailor gave me directions to my cabin. My accommodations were on the lowest deck, right next to the engine room. There were four bunk beds cramped into a small space. The cabin was dark and gloomy, and I did not have a good feeling about sleeping there.

I could hardly wait to explore the ship; I found the lounge and dining room and looked around at my fellow passengers. There were not many German-speaking people on board. Many of the passengers appeared to be refugees from the East who were emigrating.

Our journey took twelve days. We picked up quite a few passengers in Ireland. They were a happy group who liked to sing and dance. Sadly, I could not understand their Irish brogue. The crew was Italian. They spoke some English, but very little German. I kept mostly to myself wandering around the decks and reading in the small library that housed a few German books.

Soon we were on the high seas and land was no longer visible. On the third day out, heavy winds churned the water into high waves. The ship began to roll from side to side and in short order half the passengers were seasick. My stomach began to feel uncomfortable, but I was able to control my seasickness as long as I did not go below deck.

The dining room was deserted from then on. I forced myself to eat and drink a little and was glad when I could keep it all down. When everyone retired for the night I went into the lounge and slept on a couch. Sometimes I wrapped myself in a blanket and slept in one of the deckchairs. In this way I got through the next few days until the ferocity of the storm let up. Since my English was limited to just a few words, I was unable to take part in a lot of the fun going on around me. I admired a number of the handsome Italian officers and was sorry that we could not communicate.

As we got closer to America everyone's excitement grew. Like me, the passengers were probably anticipating what life would be like once we touched American soil. On the day of our arrival, October 7, everyone was on deck maneuvering for a good spot at the railing. Unfortunately, the day was overcast and foggy. There was just a hint of the New York skyline and the Statue of Liberty was shrouded in fog.

We were to dock in Hoboken, New Jersey. Belongings had been packed the night before and the middle deck was lined with every size suitcase imaginable, most of them in rather drab colors and sorry condition. Boxes and bundles were also on display and I wondered how I would locate my suitcase. A number of official looking men climbed aboard; some paperwork had to be completed before we could disembark.

I was in no particular hurry to leave the safety of the ship. What would await me? I waited until most of the passengers had left to locate my small suitcase. Then, with trembling legs, I forged my way onto American ground. I had expected to feel some wild exhilaration, but instead I was filled with apprehension. Long lines formed in front of the customs officials. Our papers were checked and occasionally someone had to open their luggage. The officials did not bother with my puny suitcase.

As soon as formalities were completed I began to search for my aunts' faces in the crowd. I could find no one that fit their description. Pretty soon I was a lonely figure in the receiving area. Most of the passengers had been met by friends or loved ones, but no one wanted to claim me.

Someone offered to take me into the city, but I did not think that was a good idea. I was eventually ushered into a waiting room. There I was shocked to see the floor strewn with cigarette butts. In East Germany, people picked up cigarette butts to recycle the tobacco that remained. I wondered at this waste.

Time moved slowly and my anxiety level rose with every passing minute. Here I was, sixteen years old, in a foreign country, unfamiliar with its language, and without money. After what seemed like an eternity, a middle aged woman in a business suit approached me and, in broken German, she explained that my aunts had hired her to bring me to the city. She had another woman and her small daughter in tow. They spoke a foreign language I could not identify.

I had little choice but to follow the woman to her huge, black car. I had never ridden in a car and felt quite excited to have this new experience. I remember the awe I felt when I first spotted the gigantic skyscrapers of Manhattan. The hustle and bustle of this big city was intimidating: The people rushing about, the taxis honking their horns and the sound of fire engines and ambulances were making me edgy.

We deposited our suitcases at the Travel Agency, located in mid-town Manhattan. For lunch, we were taken to a Horn & Hardart Automat. What an experience! The travel agent gave me a number of coins and pointed to a wall of glass doors behind which I saw all sorts of food; delicious looking sandwiches, cakes and cookies, puddings and so much more. I could not believe my eyes as I took in this abundance. Where to start? What to choose? I finally settled on a ham and cheese sandwich. When I struggled to put the coins in the slot, a kind looking woman showed me how to do it. The door popped open with a loud click, which startled me. What other marvels and surprises would reveal themselves in the days to come?

Aunt Alice and Aunt Olga arrived sometime that afternoon to escort me to their apartment. We took a taxi to 205 East 82nd Street. I found out later that my aunts rarely rode in taxis as they were extremely frugal.

The double white doors of their apartment building welcomed me to my home for the next eleven months. My aunts lived on the third floor in a one-bedroom apartment they had shared for the last twenty-five years. By combining their incomes they saved a great deal of money. This allowed them to travel the world over as well as the United States and Canada during their long summer vacations.

My aunts shared the bedroom. They each had a dresser and a single bed. The apartment had ample closet space, so there was plenty of room for my few garments. I was also given a drawer in one of the dressers. I slept on the living room couch, which was fine with me and so much better than the accommodations I had lived in for the past two years. The small kitchen had only enough space for one person.

Although my aunt's apartment was anything but luxurious by American standards, I was blown away by several things: a refrigerator, hot and cold running water, the many built-in closets, a bathroom with a shower and the small black and white television set. There were washers and dryers in the basement of the apartment building for the use of all the tenants. I could not help but think of my mother and how her life would be made easier with all these conveniences.

My aunts had a cleaning woman who came once a week. She took care of changing the linens and did the washing and ironing. I never met her, since she always came when I was at school. She had worked for my aunts for many years and they were very fond of her.

Aunt Alice was the obvious authority in this household. Eight years older than Olga, she had graduated from Hunter College with high honors and was teaching German and sometimes Spanish at a coed High School on the west side. She was attractive and supposedly had been a knockout beauty in her youth.

In contrast, Aunt Olga was the practical one who did the cooking. She had experienced many health challenges in her life. A hysterectomy, the removal of one breast, and she was a diabetic. Aunt Olga was tall and wore thick glasses. Her gray hair was cropped short. While she was not pretty, I found myself drawn to her. She exuded great warmth and had a child-like sense of humor. Aunt Alice spoke fluent German, whereas Aunt Olga spoke it well enough, but she had quite an accent and made mistakes that endeared her to me.

The next day I was given a tour of the neighborhood. The apartment building was located between 2nd and 3rd Avenue. The subway, called the El, was still running above ground on 3rd Avenue at this time, making the street dark and noisy. We went to a grocery store and I could not believe the size of it and the abundance of food it offered.

We walked to 86th Street, which at that time still had German restaurants, bakeries, and butcher stores and was referred to as Yorkville. So when I felt homesick I could simply walk to 86th Street and take in its German flavor.

After only two days I was enrolled at Julia Richman High School, an all girls' school near 68th Street on 2nd Avenue. I had hoped to go to the school where Aunt Alice taught. I surmised that my aunts did not want to expose me to a coed school in fear that I might get involved with boys. I was placed into the 11th grade according to my age. A tiny, energetic woman, who dressed glamorously, oversaw my homeroom. She wore four-inch heels to give her more height, and lots of make-up. She was Jewish and could speak some German. This helped me a lot because of my lack of English.

One of the girls in my homeroom was from Yugoslavia and also had a smattering knowledge of German. I was assigned to several English classes for foreigners, a German class where I naturally excelled, a math class and music. Everyone was kind to me and made me feel welcome. It took time to get used to the many compliments so freely given. No one had ever commented on my looks or the clothes I wore. This was evidently the American way and I liked it.

From then on life took on its routine. I worked hard to learn English because I wanted to communicate with everyone. My aunts stopped speaking German with me. In the evenings they chased me around the apartment and I had to identify everything in English. In the beginning I had difficulties with th's, w's, and v's. Aunt Olga often laughed at my pronunciation, but I was not offended.

I was given an allowance of $1.00 per week. With this money I had to buy a stamp for my weekly letter to my family (15 cents) and pay the bus fare of 15 cents if I did not want to walk to school. For some reason I was not given a key to the apartment. This puzzled me, but I did not have the nerve to inquire why. After getting home from school I waited in a small newspaper store across the street until my aunts came home. During my wait I developed a love for strawberry ice cream, which I would have as often as my small allowance permitted (one scoop cost 10 cents). I entertained myself by browsing through the magazines while licking my ice cream cone.

In the weeks to come I met my aunt's circle of friends. They were all teachers, single and except for one, they were Jewish. I addressed all of them as aunt. There was: Aunt Emma, Aunt Malvina, Aunt Sadie, Aunt Minnie and one more whose name I can't remember. They had known each other since their college days and they would get together to celebrate each other's birthday by going out to lunch in a nice restaurant. They also saw just about every Broadway show on Saturday matinees. Aunt Alice told me how all of them had helped to collect clothes for us when they sent packages to Germany.

My aunts often discussed my behavior and progress in detail with their friends over the telephone, which I especially hated when I was unable to understand what was being said.

I accompanied my aunts everywhere and whatever the occasion, I made myself useful by helping clear the table and doing the dishes. That was by far preferable to sitting still and listening to their chatter. And so I celebrated my first Thanksgiving dinner at Aunt Malvina's, who lived in the Bronx. She served a wonderful meal. Here I tasted turkey, sweet potatoes, and cranberry sauce for the first time. Seeing so much food often made me think of my family.

The weather turned colder and one Saturday my aunts took me on a shopping excursion to Alexander's, a popular department store on 34th Street. It had been years since I had gotten new clothes. I could hardly contain my excitement. I tried on shoes, a red winter coat, sweaters and skirts, which my aunts purchased for me. How proud I was of these possessions. They made me feel rich. Later on, my aunts bought me another coat, strictly to be worn on special occasions.

Aunt Alice made sure that I was exposed to culture. We visited the Metropolitan Museum, within a short walking distance from 3rd Avenue. Though I liked the museum, I found Aunt Alice's long lectures boring. She wanted to teach me so much, and I just wanted to have fun.

Despite their age (Alice was 57 and Olga 49), they had boundless energy. On many weekends we visited most of the attractions New York had to offer. There were trips to 42nd Street with its tourists, congestion and traffic; the famous Fifth Avenue with its upscale stores and St. Patrick's Cathedral; Rockefeller Center; Washington Square and Greenwich Village, where I was charmed by quaint streets and the Bohemian atmosphere; China Town, where I attempted to eat with chop sticks; and little Italy. The diversity of New York hit home when I heard foreign languages representing just about every country of the world. Since I was a foreigner myself, I felt like I should greet everyone. At times the throngs of people, who were pushing their way down crowded streets, overwhelmed me.

During the Christmas season I missed our German traditions. There was no Advent wreath and I was shocked when my aunts pulled out a scrawny, artificial Christmas tree. Where were the real candles? The colored electric lights looked pretty, but I missed the ambiance of live candles. We sang German Christmas songs and I learned a few English Christmas carols. Aunt Alice read "It was the Night before Christmas" to me. It was her ambition to translate this favored poem into German.

On Christmas Day, the next door neighbors, who had taken quite an interest in me, gifted me with a pair of ice skates. Aunt Olga immediately set to work and sewed a maroon colored ice skating skirt with matching vest. We went to the roof to take pictures, which I proudly sent to my family. Soon we took a trip to Wollman's Skating Rink in Central Park and while my aunts watched from the sidelines, I attempted to learn to skate. During that first session I mostly held onto the railing, but I eventually became quite proficient. Though I could not perform fancy moves, my skating skills were admirable. I loved gliding across the ice in time to the music, forgetting all about time and space.

During one of the ice skating sessions a boy my age tried to befriend me. He was intrigued by the fact that I was German. He could not believe it when I told him that I had chaperones with me. He was well mannered and when I introduced him to my aunts, they approved. From then on we would often meet at the skating rink. My aunts did not encourage dating and because I was not that crazy about him, I was not disappointed. I can't even remember his name.

The girls at Julia Richman High came from the five boroughs of New York City. For that reason it was difficult to form any friendships as they all rushed for subways right after school. I did befriend the girl whose family came from Yugoslavia. She lived on 2nd Avenue in a walk-up apartment. We often got together after school and I was invited to her home for several dinners and just to hang around after school.

My progress in learning the English language was astounding, and in the second semester I took a regular English class in addition to the ones being taught to foreign students. I fairly burst with pride when I received a passing grade at the end of term. My accent was slight and not typically German. Often people took me for French, which happened even more after the movie Lili, starring Leslie Caron, came out. I was told that I resembled her.

In February of 1954 I turned 17. My aunts had a small birthday party for me, the first in many years. I had gained a great deal of confidence since my arrival from Germany and blossomed with the many compliments I received on a daily basis. It no longer embarrassed me when people commented on my looks. I loved the fashion of the full skirts with crinolines underneath, sweaters that were worn backwards with small scarves tied around the neck. Nature had blessed me with a tiny waist, enhanced by wide belts that gave me the look of a tea cozy. I also put on some weight. By now I had acquired several bras. I watched other girls walk with pride, so why not me?

At my aunts' home and on outings I had to be very diplomatic. Aunt Alice wanted to be number one and the authority for everything. Though I longed to hurry down the street with Aunt Olga who had quite a stride, I had to walk next to Aunt Alice. Now and then Aunt Olga slipped me an extra dollar or a stamp for my letters. I had to be secretive about this, which troubled me. My aunts loved having me and I enjoyed their loving attention and the many luxuries offered to me.

Because Aunt Olga was a diabetic, our dinners were simple. Meats were broiled and we ate canned vegetables. I loved baked potatoes with sour cream and butter and fresh fruit for dessert. Aunt Olga loved cake, but was careful to count her calories. I did the dishes, which was an easy chore. On certain nights we watched television, which was a miraculous invention for me. My favorite shows were the musical variety shows such as Ed Sullivan, the American Band Stand and the Carol Burnett Show because they did not require much knowledge of English. Television helped me improve my English skills.

During Spring break we went by bus to Washington, D.C. to see the cherry blossoms. I loved that trip, and enjoyed touring the Capitol and White House. Here was the seat of the American government and I soaked up the atmosphere of this exciting city, so different from New York. Later in the year we took a long weekend trip to Philadelphia, where I learned much about American history.

When the weather warmed, there was an outing to Coney Island. I had only seen the ocean during my crossing and loved being near this vast body of water. It was a particularly windy day and huge waves crashed on shore. My aunts encouraged me to go to the water's edge, while they waited for me on the boardwalk. They walked with open, black umbrellas to avoid the sun, which, as a young teenager, I found a little embarrassing.

I remember fondly the first time I was treated to a Broadway show, "The Pajama Game," a musical, which was great fun. But most of all I'll never forget "Ondine," the tragic and tender love story of a water nymph, played by Audrey Hepburn. I was enthralled, and from that day on, I have been an ardent fan of this charming actress. Audrey Hepburn wore a pixie hairstyle that framed her delicate face, accentuating her charming personality. I decided on the spot that this was the hairstyle I wanted.

My trip to the beauty parlor transformed me forever. But when I first looked in the mirror I broke out in tears. My hair was not used to lying close to my head, sticking out here and there. Aunt Olga laughed and assured me that in time, I would come to love my haircut. And she was right. When my father first saw me after my return from the States, he thought that I had found my personality with this hairstyle, which he claimed made me look classy and sophisticated.

During summer vacations my aunts had taken many trips to foreign lands and across the United States. In off years, they often rented a cottage in Long Lake, NY, which was located in the beautiful Adirondack Mountains. And so when school recessed for the summer, I was told that we would spend five weeks in Long Lake. In preparation, my aunts pulled several sturdy boxes from a closet, which we packed with most of our clothes. They resembled suitcases and were fastened with thick canvas straps. A week before our trip we shipped them via parcel post to the rented cottage; this way we only needed a lightweight bag to take on the bus.

Aunt Emma would share our cottage, which had plenty of room for all of us. She joined us at the bus station for the six or so hour bus ride. When we arrived at our destination, I saw a cluster of cottages, located right on the lake, which was 14 miles long and only a little over a mile wide. Our cottage was rustic, but comfortable. Equipped with all we would need, we settled into a comfortable routine. The owner had filled the refrigerator with some basics, so there was no need to go shopping upon our arrival.

Each day I swam in the lake, tried out the rowboat which was tied to a short dock, or did a little mountain climbing across the road. It was a long walk into the small village of Long Lake and when my rowing skills improved, I was allowed to take the boat to the village. There I strolled up and down the short street, window shopped and picked up our mail from the Post Office. We prepared our own meals. Aunt Olga and Aunt Emma shared the cooking, while I was on the clean-up committee.

Several day trips took us to Tupper Lake and Lake Champlain. We also visited White Face Mountain, which had snow on top of its peak. I was glad that my aunts had advised me to bring a jacket, as it was windy and cold on top of the mountain. I reveled in these carefree days, filled with time spent in nature and reading. Occasionally a family with children arrived for a week or two and I welcomed their company.

My swimming skills improved with each day, and I dreamed of crossing the lake. I was afraid to tell my aunts, and so one morning I got up early and sneaked out of our cabin. Luckily the owner was also an early riser and he insisted that he follow me with his motor boat. And so I began my adventure. The other shore appeared so close but oh so far away when I was in the middle of the lake. At times dark clouds hung threateningly in the sky and I was so glad that someone was watching over me. I made it, but gratefully accepted a ride back. In the meantime my aunts had noticed my absence. They were standing on shore wringing their hands. I got a small scolding, but my adventure had been worth it.

It was a sad day when we prepared for our return to New York City. There was also sadness as my time in America was coming to an end. A passage had already been booked for my return to Germany in September. My family was no longer living in a displaced persons camp, and I would be going home to a new town, a new apartment, a new life. America had opened so many doors for me. It helped me to gain confidence and offered a way of life I could embrace. I secretly wished that I could return one day as an immigrant to complete my education and settle in this land of plenty.

But there was one more excursion we would undertake, a visit to the Statue of Liberty. This magnificent structure means so much to the many people who arrive daily on the American shore from foreign lands. So one Saturday we took the subway to Battery Park where we boarded the ferry to Liberty Island. The September sun was still warm and I loved standing at the bow of the ferry, feeling the wind swish through my short hair.

We leisurely strolled around the island, circling the statue and admiring the skyline of downtown Manhattan. When I gazed at this colossal edifice, standing 305 feet tall, I felt small and insignificant. Like so many immigrants, who wanted to be free and start a new life, I thought about how free I had felt during my stay in New York.

My aunts did not want to climb Miss Liberty, but I did. In those days one could still go all the way up into the torch. And so I tackled the stairs, resting at the various lookouts, which offered breathtaking vistas. My legs trembled when at last I arrived back at the bottom. The experience had been exhilarating.

I thanked my aunts for suggesting this outing. In a way it was a goodbye to New York, the city I had begun to love. On the return ferry ride I silently promised: "I will see you again, dear lady."

Aunt Alice with me
Easter in New York in the dress Aunt Olga made

Aunt Alice, me, Aunt Olga – New York 1953

Wollman Skating Rink
Central Park, New York 1954

Returning home

Leonberg - Together Again

I once again crossed the Atlantic Ocean, this time on a much larger ship, the Neptunia, which would reach Hamburg, Germany in just five days. The seas were calm and the terrible seasickness of my previous voyage was forgotten. My eighteenth birthday was only a few months away and I felt on top of the world. Some of the sophistication of my time spent in Manhattan had rubbed off. I had matured in so many ways and was proud of all I had accomplished. In just eleven months I had learned to speak, read and write English and could now converse with the English speaking passengers.

Although I was excited about seeing my family, I felt a certain apprehension. Would they like the new me? Would I like where they now lived? Most important, what would I do for the rest of my life?

I reflected on the letter I had received from my father in the spring of 1954. He had been in touch with another prisoner-of-war comrade who owned a small pharmaceutical company in Leonberg, in the state of Baden-Würtemberg, located in the south of Germany. The man offered him an administrative position, which would at last free my father from the back-breaking factory job. He also wrote that the West German government was building housing for the many displaced persons who still lingered in temporary shelters.

Vati approached the authorities who were in charge of making these assignments, and requested that our family be moved to Leonberg. By the summer of 1954 my family was able to move into their new apartment.

When we docked in Hamburg, one of Germany's largest

harbors, I was in awe of all the hustle and bustle of this old seafaring city. There was no one to meet me. After clearing customs, I got instructions on how to find the railroad station. From there I boarded a train to Stuttgart, which took approximately eight hours. I was back on German soil and being assailed by the German language, which I had not heard in a long time. I felt somewhat out of place and already missed New York.

I had gotten word to my parents as to the time of my arrival in Stuttgart. The hours on the train passed in a blur. My compartment was comfortable and I was pleased to have gotten a seat by the window. An elderly couple engaged me in conversation. They were fascinated to hear about my adventures in America and thought me very brave to have traveled so far by myself. I spent time looking at the rapidly passing landscape, much of which was rather boring. I closed my eyes and even managed several short catnaps. During the last hour my heart began to beat rapidly. I barely managed to sit still.

At last we pulled into the Stuttgart railroad station. Would my parents be there? I spotted them just as they discovered me. We ran into each others' arms and for a moment I basked in their warm embrace. Mutti did not want to let go of me. "Gittchen, we've missed you so."

My father held me by my shoulders and looked at me with appreciation. "You left as an awkward teenager and have returned a sophisticated young woman."

With arms around each other we left the train station. Vati engaged a rotund looking porter to carry my suitcases to the car he had borrowed from his boss. We piled into a gray Opel and left the parking lot.

Vati, forever the teacher, gave me a quick lesson about Stuttgart. He said, "Stuttgart is the sixth largest city in Germany and is spread across a variety of hills, some of them vineyards. There are valleys and parks – all unusual for a German city and often a surprise to visitors who primarily associate the city with its industrial reputation as the cradle of the automobile."

It was only nine miles to Leonberg. We traveled on a road

bordered by deciduous woodlands mixed with evergreens. The last stretch took us down a curving road, which almost made me sick to my stomach. "There, can you see those buildings?" Mutti said. "The first one is ours."

Shortly I would see my sisters; my heart began to race. They must have been on the lookout, for as we arrived in front of Gerlingerstrasse 38, they pounced on us like puppy dogs. They had grown so much. Bärbel had just turned fourteen and Uschi would be thirteen in January. They had shed the braids of their childhood and now had attractive short haircuts.

My sisters offered to carry my suitcases, a struggle as they climbed three flights of stairs. The bare stone stairs radiated coolness and there was an echo as we made our way to the apartment. After the huge expanses of America I was struck by the smallness of the apartment, which measured not much more than 750 square feet.

To the right was the kitchen with an electric range, a stone sink, and a kitchen cabinet that held dishes and some food staples. There was no refrigerator and no hot running water. Down the narrow hall was a small bathroom with a gas heater that was lit on Saturdays when everyone took a bath. Next, one entered the room where the family gathered to eat. Its only furnishings were a table and a corner bench and a chair. A curio cabinet held a few dishes and knick knacks. From here, a door led to a miniature balcony with a view of a building across the way, identical to ours. A small coal burning stove sat to one side. It was the only source of heat when winter arrived.

There were two more doors. One led into a sitting room where my parents slept. It held a small couch, a coffee table, an arm chair where my father read and listened to the radio. On the longest wall, a fold-out bed was hidden behind a colorful curtain. In one corner a small armoire held my parents' meager wardrobe.

The second door led to the room my sisters occupied. I was stunned when I saw how small it was. Bunk beds lined the wall where Bärbel and Uschi slept. I would be sleeping on an old divan crammed into one corner, which had seen better days. The built-in headrest made it impossible to lay flat and a large hole in the middle made sleeping uncomfortable. I eventually stuffed the hole with a pillow. Against the window sat a small desk and chair where my sisters did their homework.

The only other piece of furniture was a wardrobe. On one side were shelves that held underwear and sweaters and the other half was for hanging dresses and skirts. There simply was not enough room for any of my things, but I didn't want to think about that for now. I had forgotten that German houses and apartments did not have built-in closets.

Mutti had fixed a light supper of cold cuts, cheese and rye bread. A pot of peppermint tea complimented this simple meal. Everyone found a seat around the table and we continued getting reacquainted. I could feel myself fading. It had been a long day and though I would have liked to stay up, I took my mother's advice when she urged me to go to bed. The unpacked suitcases still stood by the divan. I just retrieved a nightgown and my toothbrush. Soon I was tucked into bed and everyone came to kiss me goodnight. The whispers and giggles of my sisters lulled me to sleep. My last thought was that family is where the heart is and I was content.

The rattling of dishes and my parents' and sisters' voices woke me the next morning. I was slightly disoriented and did not want to wake up. It was still dark and I felt a chill in the air. I pulled the covers over my head, but sleep eluded me. I dragged myself out of bed and stumbled into the bathroom. Shivering from the cold, I decided to take my 'Katzenwäsche' (a sponge bath) at a later time.

Everyone had already gathered around the breakfast table. Vati always expected us to be fully dressed and groomed before sitting down to breakfast, but since I had not unpacked my suitcase, I was permitted to stay disheveled. There was hot tea and coffee, slices of scrumptious rye bread, butter and jam. This was the usual breakfast fare. Not fully awake, I was quiet and just listened to everyone's conversation.

Soon only Mutti remained. I helped clear the table and offered to wash the breakfast dishes. This involved heating a pot of water. When the dish pan was filled, I adjusted the temperature by adding cold water. The soap suds were rinsed off and I placed the dishes on the surface next to the sink. While drying the cups and saucers, my thoughts wandered to my aunts' apartment. They, too, did not have a dishwasher, but at least there was hot running water.

Later, Mutti helped me unpack my suitcase. We hung coats and sweaters in the hall. There was also a shoe rack, and I was lucky to find a spot for my shoes. Some of my things were placed in the small wardrobe, but there was no room for everything. Mutti said, "We have some storage in the attic and all your summer clothes can go up there."

We carried the suitcases to the attic. A huge empty room to the left was strung with clothes lines. Apartment dwellers dried their laundry here on inclement days, especially during the winter months. To the right, a door led to padlocked cubicles, one for each family. There was enough space in our cubicle to store my suitcase filled with my summer clothes.

Next we went to the basement where Mutti showed me more cubicles. In ours I saw bottles of mineral water and beer, jars of marmalade and canned fruit. In one corner a huge pile of coal would provide heat in the winter; a sack of potatoes was stored in another corner. As we climbed back upstairs Mutti told me that each resident must take a turn cleaning the stairwells and windows on each floor. A sign saying "Hausordnung" (cleaning order) was hung by the apartment on duty for the week; nine apartments shared this responsibility. All residents were displaced persons, many from Prussia and Silesia. My sisters and I were the only young people in the house. Mutti told me almost all were of peasant stock. There was a slight disdain in her voice. I would meet many of them in the weeks to come.

After the apartment was in good order, Mutti invited me to go shopping with her. With no refrigeration, this was a daily chore. We armed ourselves with several shopping bags as none were provided in the stores. In 1954, Germany had few shopping centers, and large grocery stores were not in vogue as yet. On the street we joined an exodus of housewives carrying every kind of basket. I was surprised how everyone said, "Grüss Gott" (greet God), a greeting I would use over and over. Our first stop was the dairy, where our gray metal milk can was filled. Cheese and butter were also sold here. Next we stopped at the butcher where Mutti purchased soup bones and cold cuts. "Is there something special you would like?" asked my mother. I told her no.

We also stopped at the bakery for bread. I longingly looked at the delicious pastries on display. Our last stop was the green grocer who also sold canned goods and a variety of other food items. Another small store sold magazines, newspapers and various paper goods. It took over an hour to complete our errands.

I had to get used to the Schwabian dialect which was spoken by the locals. There was a slight melody to their speech and many of the words sounded different from the High German my family spoke, which immediately identified us as not being from the area.

Homemade soups were a staple. Mutti began to prepare our meal. Today it would be carrot soup, and soon delicious odors wafted through the apartment. I set the table and looked forward to my sisters' return from school. I felt a little lost and did not know what to do with myself.

My sisters, Bärbel and Uschi, arrived home around 1 p.m. and we ate our main meal at that time. I could hear their voices as they climbed up the stairs. The house was poorly built and sounds carried, especially in the stairwells. After our meal my sisters did their homework, but promised to take me on a tour of the surrounding area later that afternoon.

I learned much on our excursion. There were two more buildings identical to ours and in one of them Bärbel had a best friend by the name of Petra. The girls told me that the locals called our compound "little Moscow"; not very flattering. They also showed me the road to the center of Leonberg, the 'Römerweg' (Roman path), which was unpaved and would prove to be muddy on rainy days and throughout the winter months. We crossed over to the forest, where they showed me a path that wound its way for a long distance. We hiked for a while and I took in the scent of the woods, a smell I found exhilarating.

In the coming days I developed a routine. I helped my mother in the mornings, ran errands for her and on nice days, took a walk. In the afternoon I grabbed one of the books on loan from the local library. I wanted to get some English books and my mother promised to take me to the library in the next few days.

After I had been home for almost a week my father brought up the subject of my future. Since I had missed too many years of schooling in Germany, there was no way I could continue my education here.

I still remember it like it was yesterday. Vati was sitting at the end of the dining room table. My courage almost left me, but after taking a deep breath, I blurted out that I wanted to immigrate to America. A stunned silence followed. My father got up and walked to the window. He stood there for a long time without saying a word. I walked over to him and saw that he had tears in his eyes. We stood in silence, Vati's heartache palpable, until I could no longer bear it. At last he looked at me and said, "I would hate to lose you. America is such a long way from here, but if this is truly your wish, I will not stand in your way." He said how much I reminded him of his mother and what a good woman she had been. I longed to say something comforting to lessen the blow I had just inflicted on my father, but could not find the right words. Instead we hugged. Great relief washed over me. I could now begin to make plans for my future.

Money was a huge problem. I had none and my parents were not in a position to give me much. My father's salary barely covered their monthly expenses and often there was nothing left by the 25th of the month.

My plan was to get a job with the American occupation in order to keep fluent with my English. This required a trip to Stuttgart, which I planned for the very next day. The employment office that hired German nationals to fill various jobs was located on 'Königstrasse,' right in the middle of Stuttgart. Thankfully, the day was sunny, because I had to walk for three quarters of a mile. My heart fluttered as I entered the store front office. Women sat at several desks. I approached the nearest one. The young, friendly looking woman asked how she could help me. My disappointment was enormous when I learned that I had to be 18 years old before I could be hired. Typing a minimum of 35 wpm was another requirement.

My 18th birthday was still months away. On my way back to the bus stop I devised a plan to acquire typing skills. I passed many stores displaying beautiful clothes and several restaurants that looked most inviting. With just enough money for my bus fare, I squared my shoulders and silently said, "Some day!"

Fall was coming to an end. The forest across the road, no longer ablaze with color, showed just a few brown-yellow leaves clinging to barren branches. I was glad for the evergreen trees; Mother Nature would not look completely ravished.

The month of November ushered in gray and misty days. Since the surrounding roads were not paved, when it rained they were mired in mud. On those days our shoes were badly soiled. We removed them before entering the apartment and placed them on the stone sink in the kitchen. My sisters and I took turns cleaning our father's shoes. We used water to remove the caked-on mud. After drying them, shoe polish was applied, and we buffed them with a soft rag to a pristine shine. My sisters and I agreed that this was our least favorite chore.

One day Vati brought home a decrepit-looking upright typewriter. I was glad to have it, for I needed to practice my typing. It was also good to have something to do. Day after day I sat at the dining room table pounding the keys; several of which stuck. Without a book of instructions, I found it difficult to learn the ten-finger touch system. No matter how hard I tried, I could not help looking at my fingers. I typed letters to my aunts in New York and made up stories. Progress was slow and many a day I wanted to give up. Mutti did not complain about the noisy typewriter; I was grateful for that. I began to copy passages from books and my speed increased slightly. But because I was not using the touch system I made many mistakes and I knew that these would count against me.

One day ran into the next and I looked forward to the weekends when everyone was at home. Although my mother cleaned the apartment on a daily basis, Saturday morning was set aside for an extra "big cleaning". My father insisted that we help our mother; we wore aprons to protect our clothes. I volunteered to clean the small bathroom.

I couldn't wait to take the area rug from our sitting room downstairs. It was not heavy, but cumbersome to handle. Bärbel helped me to the basement, where a door led to the back of the house. We hung the rug on a large iron rafter and I began to beat it with abandon, wielding a rug beater. I loved doing this. I exerted lots of energy whacking the rug, all the while getting rid of anxiety and frustrations. I noticed others doing the same.

I was especially intrigued by a tiny, older woman wearing a bright blue kerchief that contrasted sharply with her otherwise drab clothing. I remembered how women of all ages in America dressed in vibrant colors. No bright colors were worn here. Many widows wore black for the rest of their lives. The woman appeared to take great pleasure beating her small rug. I wondered what she was angry about.

Saturday was also the day we got to take a bath. The gas heater was lit in late afternoon, as it took two hours to get hot water. The tank only held enough to fill two bathtubs; my parents shared one and we girls the other. Because we lived on the top floor, the noise of running water could be heard throughout the house. There was a gurgling sound in the pipes, audible when the tub was filled and drained. House rules required that all noise cease by 10 p.m.. We washed our hair in the sink on another day. This, too, was time consuming because water had to be heated in the kitchen. Thankfully, we all had short hair.

In the weeks to come I also learned how difficult it was to do laundry. Mutti sent sheets and tablecloths to a laundry, as they were too cumbersome to handle. Although there was a laundry room in the basement, my mother preferred to do our wash in the kitchen. Wash day was actually a two-day affair. A huge black pot was filled with water and brought to a boil with some type of laundry detergent. Underwear and all whites bubbled for several hours. Mutti had a scrubbing board and a large wooden spoon, with which she lifted the steaming pieces of underwear, shirts and other small items of clothing. They were then scrubbed and placed in a tub of cold water to rinse. This process was repeated twice. I helped wring out the wash and found out that my wrists were just as fragile as my mother's, and I had difficulty getting all the water out. Next, everything was put in a large basket, which we carried to the attic because the weather was no longer conducive for hanging the wash outside.

Many of the cloth lines were already filled with others' wash, but we found enough room to hang ours. I handed the clothespins to my mother while she expertly fitted everything on two long lines. We often draped damp wash all over the apartment to speed up the drying process. The colored wash was done on another day when the whole process was repeated. There were not enough hours to fit white and colored wash into one day.

The large basket of laundry then had to be ironed, and I loved doing that. Mutti showed me how to iron Vati's shirts, as well as blouses, and in time I excelled at this chore. I now understood why we did not change our clothes on a daily basis and why Vati insisted we wear aprons around the house.

As time went by I became more restless. The sameness of each day began to fray my nerves. With no TV for entertainment, evenings were long and boring. I did play "Rummey," a game played with two decks of cards. Reading was another form of entertainment, but even that got tiresome. Vati was usually sitting in his easy chair listening to classical music on the radio. From this exposure we all learned to love Beethoven, Tchaikovsky, Mozart and Brahms. He also read his treasured small volumes of poetry by Johann Wolfgang von Goethe. These he had with him throughout the war and in the prisoner-of-war camp in Russia. Many of the passages were underlined, revealing his thoughts during those difficult days.

We celebrated Advent on the four Sundays before Christmas. Families gathered near the Advent wreath and each Sunday a candle was lit; first one, then two until all four were burning on the fourth Sunday.

My father was not a religious man, but he liked to keep certain traditions. The Advent Season was one of them, when he would bring home a large wreath made of fresh pine. I loved to sink my face into the pine needles, taking in the scent of the forest. He would purchase several yards of bright red ribbon. The ribbon, about 2 ½ inches wide, was cut into four equal pieces and fastened to the wreath. A hook was already in place on the ceiling and Vati gathered the four ribbons, tying them into a bow so the wreath could hang. Then four fat, red candles were placed in candle holders that were stuck into the thick wreath.

On Sunday all lights were doused, and we reverently followed the flame of the candle as it danced in the dark room. There was a little bit of magic when all was silent. This reverie was only broken when Mutti brought in a tray of home baked Christmas cookies, a rare treat since we seldom had sweets.

Before we knew it, Christmas had arrived. We had not been together as a family in four years and our spirits were soaring. My parents' room had been locked since the week before Christmas. My sisters and I took turns peeking through the key hole in hopes of discovering its secrets. Heilig Abend (Christmas Eve) had always been special. In Germany, an Angel called Christkind (Christ Child), brings the presents. She flies through the sky and Santa is her helper. No need for a fireplace, since she comes in right through the window.

My sisters were on school holiday and my father was off from work. Delicious odors poured forth from our tiny kitchen, permeating every crevice of our small apartment. Polnische Sosse (Polish Sauce), the special meal only served on Christmas Eve, was brewing in the kitchen. A large pot, filled with water and soup greens and a piece of smoked meat, was bubbling on the stove. While it simmered on low for most of the morning, a spicy, unsweetened Pfefferkuchen (spice cake) soaked in dark, sweet Malt Beer. Later this concoction was joined with the stock from the soup pot. The Pfefferkuchen mixture turned the stock into a thick dark sauce. Mutti stirred it often. Sauerkraut, boiled potatoes and Weisse Wurst (white veal sausages) would be served with this sauce. It must have been a recipe from Silesia, since I rarely met anyone familiar with this dish.

My sisters and I were restless, driving our mother crazy. In late afternoon she insisted that we go to the local Lutheran church for the traditional Christmas Eve service. We bundled up and bounced down the three flights of stairs, full of whispers and giggles. The stairwell smelled of the meal my mother was cooking. Other aromas wafted from other apartments.

It took close to thirty minutes to walk to the village church. We were chilled to the bone by the time we reached our destination. The church offered a welcome respite from the cold. The service was already in progress and we quietly slipped into the closest pew to the rear of the church. Much of what went on has escaped my memory. Was it holy, was the Christmas story a revelation? I think we felt some awe, some wonder as we quietly walked home. Stars were beginning to sparkle in a black sky and to our delight, snowflakes began to fall.

A big surprise awaited us when we returned home. Our brother, Peter, had decided at the last minute to join us for Christmas. He got a ride from a fellow police student and could only spend two days with us. It was good to see him. He had grown into a handsome young man, and we girls admired his muscles and strong build. Peter looked me over with a critical eye. I was not sure if he approved of the new me. He had brought a heavy sleeping bag, since we did not have a bed for him.

Soon it was time to eat and six of us crowded around the small table. My sisters' eyes often focused on the closed door. I, too, wondered what surprises awaited us. Tradition demanded that the girls cleared the table and washed the dishes before the festivities could proceed. Though I was no longer required to help with this chore (I had put in my years of duty), I joined Bärbel and Uschi to hurry up the process. My sisters had lovely voices and soon the kitchen was filled with the sounds of Christmas carols.

Finally the big moment arrived! Vati opened the door. The room was dark, except for the light coming from the Christmas tree, adorned in silver with white, live candles. We stood in wonder, admiring the beauty of our tree. Still standing near the open door, we sang 'O Du Fröhliche, oh Du Seelige' (O Sanctissima), sometimes referred to as the Mariner's Hymn. It is an old carol that is also sung in American churches. We hugged each other and exchanged wishes for a Merry Christmas.

Presents were not wrapped. Instead each person had a designated spot where their gifts were spread. We each received a large Christmas plate filled with sweets; an apple, marzipan and home baked Christmas cookies. Our brother made the rounds, trying to get us to trade for his favorite sweet. He was quite charming about it and sulked when we refused his pleas. Money was tight and our gifts were of a practical nature, but we were pleased. Most of all, we enjoyed being a family, sitting around the tree and reminiscing about past Christmases.

A week later, we celebrated Sylvester (New Year's Eve). Vati purchased colorful paper hats and noisemakers. After a simple dinner we donned our hats, which seemed to change our personalities. My sisters and I acted quite silly, laughing uncontrollably until Vati told us to calm down. Later that evening we ate Mohnklösse (Poppy seed dumplings), a traditional Silesian recipe guaranteed to bring good luck for the New Year. Vati prepared them the day before. I still don't know why they were called dumplings. The recipe called for finely ground poppy seeds mixed with raisins and almonds. Layers of this mixture and white bread that had been soaked in milk were placed in a large bowl. This concoction was soaked with sugar and a little bit of rum. It had to sit overnight so all the flavors could combine. One needed to develop a taste for this dish, but I was willing to try it.

Another tradition had everyone excited, Bleigiessen (pouring of lead). Packages of small lead pieces were purchased. They came in many shapes, mostly animals. A flat, metal spoon was included. We each selected a piece of lead and took turns melting it over the flame of a candle. As soon as the lead was liquid, we quickly dumped it into a bowl of cold water. With much debate, we attempted to analyze the intricate configuration that quickly took shape, guaranteed to foretell what was in store for us in the New

Year. This took up quite a bit of time and before long it was 11 p.m.

Vati retired to his easy chair and was waiting for the broadcast of Beethoven's Ninth Symphony, a New Year's Eve tradition. Throughout the concert he sat still, deep in thought. We entertained ourselves with a game of Sorry, and Mutti joined us. During the last, rousing movement of the symphony, Vati invited us to listen to the spectacular chorale finale, which proclaimed peace among mankind. Midnight was near and we girls began to blow our noisemakers. Although it was frigid outside, we opened the balcony door as the church bells ushered in the New Year. When I turned in for welcome sleep, my thoughts drifted to what the coming year would hold for me. Hopefully a job!

January brought a stretch of frigid weather. The apartment was so cold in the morning that I did not want to get out of bed. I felt sorry for my sisters and Vati, who had a long walk to school and work. Overnight, ice flowers had formed on the windows. They were so delicate and their intricate configurations fascinated me; when I blew on them they dissolved.

One day a thick package arrived for me from the American Consulate. There was a ton of paperwork to fill out for my application for immigration. I took this opportunity to practice my typing skills. There were also forms my aunts needed to complete, since they had agreed to be my sponsors. I wrote them a long overdue letter.

I increased my daily typing sessions to several hours a day. I had dubbed the typewriter "the black monster," and let out some not so nice expletives when I made mistakes. While my speed had improved, I was still far away from typing 35 wpm.

A gymnast competition had been set for the end of the month at the local 'Turnhalle' (a large hall for sports activities). My sisters had friends that would participate, and they invited me to join them. We bundled up and walked the mile or so to the 'Turnhalle'. A large crowd had already gathered and the hum of voices filled the hall. I was introduced as the big sister from America, a name that followed me from then on.

The crowd settled on narrow benches to the left and right. I was reluctant to find a seat because I felt uncomfortable among so many strangers. Instead, I stationed myself near the entrance. I noticed a young woman to the left of me. She was about two inches taller than me. Her hair, a dark blond, was fashionably cut. She had a prominent nose that made her look determined. We began a conversation. I learned that her name was Adele Weiss. She lived nearby with her parents and an older brother. She worked in Stuttgart as a secretary, but her passion was singing. She dreamed of becoming an opera singer. I was in awe of so much ambition.

Before we parted, Adele invited me to her home the next Sunday afternoon, to listen to classical music. I was elated! A friend; how wonderful! I counted the days until Sunday, excited to get away from my monotonous life. My journey took me across the Römerweg and through a section of Leonberg. Adele lived in a tiny house that was surely hundreds of years old. The ceilings were low and the floors seemed to slant downwards. I met Adele's parents, who were refugees from East Prussia. They were short in stature. I wondered how they grew such a tall daughter. Adele's brother also put in an appearance. Karl was an Engineering student. He, too, was on the short side, but had an attractive face and a lovely smile.

Adele had banned everyone from the living room. She proudly showed me her phonograph and a collection of long-playing records. After her mother served us coffee and a home baked apple cake, we settled down to an afternoon concert. I got to choose the record and after much back and forth, settled on Rachmaninoff's Piano Concerto No. 1. Adele carefully lifted the record from its sleeve and placed it on the turntable.

The rousing opening shook me to the core. The walls of the small living room seemed to vibrate and the small windows trembled. There were some wonderful slow passages in the second movement, and I began to recognize the "Leitmotiv." Not a word was spoken until the last sounds of the concert ebbed away. I was filled with love and longing, grateful for this opportunity to have shared this experience with my new friend.

From then on we met often. Our friendship meant much to me. Here was someone I could use as a sounding board, someone who questioned our existence, someone who had dreams.

During the week Mutti and I tuned into a radio station that played light, classical music. We heard Strauss waltzes and the music of Franz Lehar, who composed many light operettas. When my body got stiff from sitting at the typewriter, I skipped and danced around the room. One time I grabbed Mutti and we danced to the strains of the Vienna Woods. Mutti was light on her feet, and she confided to me that she had wanted to be a dancer in her younger years. Sadly, her dreams were squashed when her father died tragically when she was just sixteen.

One evening the radio broadcast an hour of dance music. My sisters and I begged our father to teach us how to dance. He needed little coaxing because he, too, loved to dance. Vati demonstrated the graceful movements of a waltz with Mutti. Their posture was perfect and although there was little space, they managed to waltz around the room. In my mind's eye I saw them in ballroom attire and it made me sad that they no longer went dancing. Soon it was our turn and Vati attempted to teach us by repeating, "one two three, one two three." I felt clumsy and stepped on Vati's slippered feet a number of times. Just as I got the hang of it, the music stopped. Next Vati taught us a foxtrot, and then a polka. We jumped around the room. Soon our neighbor from below banged on the ceiling. Sadly, our dance lessons came to a halt.

My parents were avid readers, as were my sisters. Mutti went to the library on a weekly basis. When given the opportunity, I welcomed the diversion and accompanied her. I helped with the heavy load of books, which we carried in linen cloth satchels.

The library was located on the main road in Leonberg which we reached by way of the Römerweg. At the library I met Frau Doctor Hollister, who had a Ph.D. in library science. Everyone addressed her as Frau Doctor. Mutti proudly introduced me as the daughter who had been to America. We shook hands and I was surprised when Frau Doctor addressed me as Fräulein Grunwald, instead of by my first name, as children were usually addressed.

I inquired about books in English and Frau Doctor led me to a shelf that had an amazingly large selection. While I decided on my reading material, Mutti was engaged in animated conversation with Frau Doctor Hollister. She adored my mother and looked forward to her frequent visits. They spoke High German, shared similar backgrounds, and had a love for books. She reserved the latest best sellers for my mother, knowing how quickly they would be returned.

I chose a Hemingway book and "Of Mice and Men," by Steinbeck. It surprised me that there was a charge for each book, and I wondered how this fit into my parents' budget. Our hunger for mental stimulation satisfied, we left the library in an upbeat mood.

My milestone birthday arrived at last. The day before, it began to snow. I watched from the window as snowflakes gently floated from the sky. It did not look like the snow would stick, but soon a layer of white covered the ground. The flakes got thicker and it appeared as if a curtain was coming down from the sky.

I wanted to play in the snow, but did not have the right clothes. None of my family had boots and all I brought from the States were a pair of ugly see-through galoshes. However, my curiosity overcame my vanity and I told Mutti I would do the shopping. By the time I got downstairs the snow was piling up. I had fun creating a path with my footprints. Women wrapped in warm scarves were already shoveling the sidewalks. My shopping list was not long. I was home in no time. I put my basket down in front of our building and made several snow balls. The snow was wet and did not want to stick, and I could not build a snowman. I silently thanked Mother Nature for dressing up the landscape in time for my birthday.

That night I fell asleep envisioning a job. My first thought upon waking was that I was now eighteen, ready to take on the world. My birthday cake sat on the table and there was even a small gift. Everyone hugged me and wished me a wonderful new birth year. I was all smiles, grateful for my family and looking forward to a wonderful future.

Mutti fixed potato pancakes for our lunch, a favorite of mine. She spent a long time in the kitchen grating the raw potatoes. Her efforts yielded a large bowl of shredded potatoes that she mixed with a raw egg and some flower. When my sisters came home from school Mutti heated the frying pan with a little oil, which sputtered as she dropped small amounts of the mixture into the frying pan. I watched as three small pancakes took shape, breathing in the delicious aroma. Mutti brought a large platter filled with crispy pancakes to the table, which we ate with apple sauce. We saved the birthday cake for the evening so my father could share in the celebration. It was a most satisfying day.

Three days later it was my mother's birthday. She did not want to bake another cake as enough was left over from mine. I felt sad that I did not have a gift for her, but wrote her a note in which I offered to do all the housework for that day. I wanted her to relax, read, sleep – whatever would give her joy. She found it difficult to not follow her usual routine, but I was firm and forced her to let me do everything. Mutti would not admit it, but I could tell that loafing agreed with her.

As it happened, it was our turn for 'Hausordnung'. I heated a pot of water to add to the ice cold water in the pail. Armed with a large rag, Windex and newspapers for cleaning the windows, I climbed up to the attic floor. The stairwell was so cold that before long my hands were beet red. Because of muddy conditions outdoors, the stairs were in a deplorable condition. I had to change the dirty water several times. I worked my way down each floor and several neighbors opened their doors, surprised when they saw me instead of my mother. I greeted them with the obligatory 'Grüss Gott,' to which they responded without a smile or another word.

On the second floor, I ran into Frau Kovinsky, a widow from East Prussia. She was about to walk her beautiful dog, Petro, an Irish setter. I allowed Petro to smell me before I dared to stroke his rich red fur. This gesture endeared me to Frau Kovinsky. Petro and I became friends and his tail wagged wildly whenever our paths crossed.

At last I finished washing all the stairs, even the ones that lead to the basement. Next the windows had to be cleaned. They looked fine to me except for spots on the outside. Luckily, they opened, allowing me to clean with ease. I examined my work and liked what I saw. This same procedure would have to be repeated the next day, since we had this duty all week.

During the next few days I put in one last effort to hone my typing skills. Not knowing if my test would be in German or English, I copied text from Hemingway's "For Whom the Bell Tolls." I loved this book and recalled the day I saw the movie in Berlin, which affected me so deeply. It was easier to type English because the words were not so long.

I kept postponing going to the employment office in Stuttgart and realized that I was afraid – afraid of not passing the typing test, afraid of not getting a job. My parents and my friend Adele encouraged me, "Just do it!"

And so the following Monday I dredged up every ounce of courage and went to Stuttgart. By now I was familiar with the route. I was a bundle of nerves.

A little sunshine would have helped my mood, but the skies were heavy with grey clouds. It even looked like it might snow.

I took a deep breath and entered the employment office. Inside it was pleasantly warm. There were only a few people waiting on chairs and no line at the reception desk. The young woman manning this station greeted me with a smile and handed me several forms to fill out. She directed me to a desk where I sat and comfortably answered all the questions.

Next, I was asked to show proof of age. Luckily I had brought my passport. I also took this opportunity to leave my letters of recommendation. More waiting. Fifteen minutes seemed like a long time, but when I heard my name, I wished it had been longer. The dreaded typing test awaited me.

I was led to another room with several desks, each with a large typewriter. I had ten minutes to practice. The typewriter was a much newer model than I had been used to and none of the keys were sticking. A stack of paper sat next to the typewriter and I rolled in one of the sheets. My touch was tentative, almost like I was afraid to hit the keys. My right leg performed involuntary jerks

I didn't know how to stop.

Practice ended – the test began. Another employee handed me a letter on a stand and told me to copy it. It was in English, and that was fine with me. Breathe deeply, I told myself. Silently I counted to ten and nodded my head, indicating that I was ready. My shaking hands flew over the keys. I knew I was making some mistakes, but my focus was on completing this task. The bell rang much too soon and I stopped typing.

Prayer was not yet part of my life. All I could think of was "please, please let me have passed the test." I was so focused on this wish that I almost did not hear my name when it was called.

This time I met with an older woman who had the sweetest smile. "You passed your typing test, barely," she said "but hopefully you will improve your speed in time." In a kind voice she told me, "We like that you speak such excellent English, which will serve us well. Unfortunately, we do not have a job opening at the present time."

My disappointment was palpable; I was close to tears. Frau Müller, (I saw her name plaque), sensed my despair and tried to comfort me. She intimated that new developments were taking place, and said a job would turn up soon. I would surely hear something within the next few weeks.

Since we did not have a telephone, I left my father's business phone number. I suppressed my tears as I departed, disappointed, but with a ray of hope in my heart.

My mother's only sister, Fee Haase and family, lived in Stuttgart. It had been years since I last saw her. When Mutti and I received an invitation for afternoon coffee, I looked forward to reacquainting myself with this part of my family. I was especially curious to see cousin Bodo.

On our bus ride to Stuttgart, Mutti filled me in on the Haase's journey. It was fascinating how it ran parallel to that of my family. Like my father, Onkel Heinz Haase had served in the German Army and ended up in a prisoner of war camp in Russia. He returned to East Germany in 1949, where he found work in Oschatz and later in East Berlin. I don't know details, but he was also interrogated by the KGB on several occasions and feared for his safety and the safety of his family. Like us, they left everything behind and escaped to West Berlin in early 1954.

Tante Fee's family were members of the "Reformed Church," who helped them to reach West Germany. They first landed in Bavaria and later moved to Stuttgart, where an old colleague found an excellent position for Onkel Heinz, who was an architect/builder, a profession always in demand.

The Haase family lived not far from the main railroad station. A steep incline had us huffing and puffing as we made our way uphill. We were no longer cold when we arrived at the apartment building. The climb to the third floor further added to our being out of breath when we rang the bell to their apartment.

Tante Fee embraced me with a warm hug. She looked much like I remembered her: about my mother's height, with blond hair that was fashionably coiffed. And she had a lovely smile and an infectious, innocent laugh, Onkel Heinz, who towered over her, was lean and wore glasses. His demeanor was more serious; no smiles from him. He had extended his lunch hour to greet us, but had to return to work shortly after we arrived.

I was impressed by the high ceilings of my aunt's apartment, which gave it the appearance of spaciousness. Although they had not lived here long, the apartment was well furnished. My mother must have envied their large kitchen with all its counter space. In the center of the living room, that had huge windows, was a dining room table, set with a linen tablecloth and exquisite china.

My mother went by the name of Doris and I was surprised when Tante Fee called her Dora. In her childhood Mutti went by the name of Dorothea, shortened to Dora. I liked the ring of that. Coffee was served from a delicate china pot and there was even whipped cream. Cake in the middle of the week! What a rare treat for my mother and me.

Tante Fee entertained me with stories about her time in Breslau, where she studied costume design. She was employed at the Breslau Opera House and I could see how this had been her passion. Tante Fee proudly showed me a sketchbook filled with delightful drawings of women in colorful costumes.

The doorbell rang, and my cousin Bodo bounced into the apartment. I had last seen him when he was ten. He had grown considerably. While he was wolfing down his second piece of cake, he talked about his studies. He planned to follow in his father's footsteps and become an architect/builder.

On our way home, Mutti explained how Onkel Heinz and Vati had different political and world outlooks. They did not see eye to eye on many subjects, especially not on religion. The Haases were deeply religious, whereas my father was an Agnostic. This explained why our families socialized only on rare occasions. However, I need to mention that during my parent's senior years, Tante Fee and Onkel Heinz performed many wonderful deeds for them when they were in dire need of assistance.

Leonberg Markplatz

My family, December 1954

Me and my friend Adele

Hajo's Wedding July 1955

In the weeks that followed there was a longing in me I could not explain. I was tired of grey skies and inclement weather. Our supply of potatoes was alarmingly low, and since they were such a staple in our diet it was a concern. Others still had jars of canned vegetables and fruit in their storage room, but this was not the case with us. My mother never learned the art of canning, so did not take advantage when fruits and vegetables were in season. We made do with canned goods that were available from stores.

One evening I noticed my father had a mysterious look about him when we sat down to eat our evening meal. I pressed him for news. He seemed to enjoy keeping me in suspense, but relented at last. With a smile on his face, Vati told me, "You'll have a job soon! They want you to come to Stuttgart for another interview." I jumped up from the table and let out a victory cry, then hugged my parents and sisters until they hurt.

The interview went well. A new Refugee Act was permitting a large number of people from Eastern European countries to immigrate to the United States. There were instructions to report to Olgastrasse 13 where the American Consulate had rented an old building that would house the temporary Refugee Investigation Division.

Words can't describe how I felt. The wait had been so long. I could finally look forward to earning a salary. But for now, I still needed my parents' support. Payday would not be until the end of the month.

My job began on April 13, a Wednesday, because of Easter. Easter was a big holiday weekend in Europe. No one worked on Good Friday or on the Monday after Easter. Throughout Lent everything had been somber. The radio played only serious music and people walked around with earnest faces. That changed with Easter morning when church bells rang and a joyful countenance was back in vogue.

Everyone was home for the long weekend and it was difficult to find privacy. My sisters retired to their room and read on their beds. My father had his spot in the living room. I didn't know where to go.

As I did so often, I helped my mother with household chores. Stores would be closed on Monday, so we did a big shopping on Saturday to stock up for the long weekend. When we got home I watched her bake a 'Streusselkuchen' (crumb cake) for Easter Sunday. We also colored eggs, which my parents hid around the apartment on Easter Sunday. They were nestled in small baskets with chocolate bunnies and other sweets.

On this long weekend I managed to meet my friend, Adele. She shared in my excitement about the upcoming job. Adele worked in Stuttgart and we studied the bus schedule to see if we could ride the same bus to work.

The majority of the Baden-Württemberg population is Catholic. If anything, we would be Lutherans; both of my sisters were confirmed in that faith. But when people flocked to church on Easter Sunday, we were at home listening to an organ concert on the radio. In later years I became a huge fan of organ music.

The German people are walkers, and take every opportunity to be outdoors. On Sunday afternoons Vati insisted that we join him for a walk in the woods, where a variety of paths led to various destinations. People walked their dogs in the forest; little dogs and big ones. German Shepherds and Golden Retrievers seemed to be the preferred breed. They often ran without a leash, but their owners watched them carefully to make sure they didn't bother us. There was a faint veil of green on trees and bushes; a harbinger of what would soon be a sea of color.

April 13 could not arrive fast enough to suit me. I rose at 6 a.m., which felt like the middle of the night. Mutti had already set the breakfast table and as soon as I had my turn in the bathroom, I gratefully drank a hot cup of tea. The stove had not yet kicked in and it was chilly. Mutti packed a brown paper bag with a sandwich for my lunch which sat next to my place setting. My attire had been carefully planned the night before. A black skirt with a baby-blue sweater set, adorned with a small, colorful scarf, made me look professional. I wore no make-up, except for a touch of lipstick in a mauve color.

Everyone wished me luck as I left the apartment. It was still dark and quite cool. I made it to the bus stop in good time and was pleased that Adele had managed to save me a seat. The bus was filled with people like me, who were going to work, as well as a sprinkling of students.

I was on pins and needles, unable to focus on anything. Adele attempted to calm me without much success. I had no idea how long it would take me to get to Olgastrasse and wished that I had taken a trial run. It turned out that I had plenty of time, though it took a good twenty minutes of brisk walking to reach my destination.

My work place was located next to the American Consulate. I hesitated before entering the building, taking deep breaths to give me courage. This was after all my first real job.

A large entry hall with rooms to the left and right greeted me. All was quiet, but when I knocked on the closest door, a loud voice yelled "Enter," and I met Master Sgt. William Sadek, Jr. He was a stocky man in his mid-forties. A mustache gave him a bit of a sinister look, but his eyes told another story. He had a deep, sonorous voice; I could tell he was used to giving orders. I introduced myself and he told me that I was early. "Have a seat until the others arrive. I don't want to have to repeat everything twice." His gruff manner intimidated me just a little.

Soon a troupe of boisterous soldiers appeared. They were from the CIC (Counter Intelligence Corps), which had a small base in Stuttgart. Their assignment for the foreseeable future was under the supervision of Sgt. Sadek. They were a lot more confident than I was, and acted relaxed and carefree.

Sgt. Sadek invited us to follow him upstairs where he showed us a number of rooms furnished with several desks. There was also a small kitchen with a table and chairs, a miniature refrigerator and a stove. Here we could deposit our lunch and make tea or coffee when desired.

There were more offices on the next level, but they were not needed at this time. Bathroom facilities were also located on that floor. Sgt. Sadek was expecting more people, but decided to begin making room assignments. I was shown to a desk that would be mine for the duration of my job. It held a typewriter, in-and-out boxes, a stack of white paper, and pens and pencils in an ordinary looking cup holder. I stowed my purse in one of the empty drawers and waited for further instructions.

Two young women arrived. One was American, of Eurasian descent, with ebony hair that fell like a curtain down her back. Two barrettes held her hair away from her face. She wore glasses and her eyes were kind. The other young woman was German. She was on the thin side and appeared high-strung.

Sgt. Sadek ushered us into a large room that had been set up as a conference room. He asked us to take a seat around an oblong table with a dozen chairs. It was then that I realized that this would be my new world, a job that would be important.

"Welcome" he said. "I am Sgt. Sadek and in charge of this division. You will be under my supervision for the duration of your employment here. All questions and concerns should be directed to me. My office is located on the ground floor and my door is always open. Soon you will get to know each other and since we are small in number, I would like you to think of us as a family." He took a deep breath. "You will be handling many files that contain intimate and personal information. Though you will never be in contact with the subjects, please be aware that this is privileged information, to remain confidential, and is not to leave these premises. I count on your discretion." As a last reminder he told us to be on time, to call if we are unable to come to work, and to be focused. We also learned that we had a fifteen minute break in the morning and afternoon, and that our lunch hour was forty-five minutes long.

Sgt. Sadek then directed us to our various offices. I was delighted when the American woman was assigned to my room. Her name was Jean Pearce, and she was the wife of an enlisted man who had been drafted before he could complete his Masters degree in English Literature. She, too, was a college graduate. She and her husband lived off base because they wanted to immerse themselves in the German culture. Jean had studied German in college and asked if I would be willing to help her improve her language skills. I told her a little about myself and was pleased when she complimented me on my proficiency in English. For the moment, there was nothing to do, so we continued to chat. Although I had not spoken English in almost five months, our conversation flowed with ease.

At lunch time introductions and lots of hand shaking took place. The German girl's name was Siggie. She giggled a lot and was in heaven to be among so many male soldiers. I could tell that she was an expert in flirting, something that was foreign to me.

All the soldiers from the CIC were recent graduates from prestigious schools such as Yale, Harvard and Princeton. I thought I would like them all except for a wiry young man with a high-pitched voice. He called himself Erwin, came from Massachusetts, and though I didn't know much about American accents, I could tell that he used a different inflection. He appeared to be a snob, which he covered up with a nervous laugh.

There was one young man who made my heart race. His name was David, and he looked to be over six feet tall and had dark blue eyes, a deep, melodious voice and beautiful hands, all attributes I admired in a man.

There were no restaurants or shops nearby and only Jean and I had come prepared, so Sgt. Sadek sent out for sandwiches. After lunch everyone drifted back to their offices. I couldn't believe my luck when David joined Jean and me in ours. He obviously wanted to get to know us. My experience with boys and men had been very limited. I was shy and let Jean do most of the talking.

David was from Michigan and had graduated from Princeton. He was looking forward to seeing more of Europe and explained since his duties at CIC Headquarters were light, it was easy to get weekend passes. He and his friends had already been to Paris.

Sgt. Sadek came into our office with an armload of files and showed us what our duties would be. The files contained documents, forms, and letters – in short, the life story of people with no face. Jean and I would work on these files after the young men had studied them. At times investigative work was required. Much of the information was in German, but there were also documents like marriage licenses and work records in other languages. Sgt. Sadek asked if I could translate German to English and I told him that I would love to give it a try. He had already ordered an excellent German/English dictionary.

On this first day not much was accomplished. Before we left I took the time to look around. The house, which once must have been a private residence, had been stripped of all décor. There were no window treatments, no pictures on the walls. Jean promised to bring in a plant to dress up our stark office. I wracked my brain. What could I contribute?

The soldiers were picked up by a small army bus at closing time. No such luxury awaited the rest of us. Jean headed for a street car stop on Königstrasse. I walked with her part of the way. This gave us the opportunity to speak German. Jean's accent was charming.

There was a spring in my step as I made my way to my bus stop. A feeling of well-being embraced me; I could not seem to wipe the smile from my face. I was well pleased with the turn my life was taking.

Spring unfolded in all its splendor as Mother Nature splashed delicate greens on trees that had lain barren over the winter months. Tulips, daffodils, and hyacinths popped up in neighborhood gardens. I especially liked the forsythia bushes that brightened the landscape with their sunny yellow color. In the forest I spotted dainty lily of the valley with their tender white bells. Temperatures were warming up and the sun shone more often. It was as if everyone and everything was being reborn.

Work went well. My typing skills were more than adequate, since I mostly filled in forms. Occasionally, a letter needed to be typed, documents needed to be translated and copied. Sgt. Sadek was right when he said that we would become like a family. Jean and I were especially close. We liked to refer to the enlisted men as "the boys," for they certainly acted like boys. They popped in and out of our office, making small talk and trying to get me to blush; an easy feat. Many of their jokes went right over my head.

It occurred to me that we were all here on an interim stop. For the boys from the CIC, it was a time to get away from their boring duties at their base. For me it was an opportunity to improve my English skills, which I knew would be so important when I immigrated to America. I had not heard anything from the American Consulate, and wondered if my aunts had completed the forms for my sponsorship. For Jean it was a way to stay busy and to earn some money. She was kind enough to supply me with reading material. I read "The Great Gatsby" by Fitzgerald and several books by Hemingway. Hemingway's short and crisp sentences made for an easy read.

It was difficult to hide that I had a huge crush on David, the most handsome of the young men. He treated me with respect, and when, after two weeks on the job, he was assigned to our office, I was in heaven. His desk was right across from mine, and in the beginning it was difficult for me to concentrate on my work. Just hearing his deep voice gave me the jitters. These were new feelings, and I didn't know how to process them.

Payday arrived at the end of the month. My very first pay check was small. Not much was left over after I purchased the monthly bus ticket and paid some money back to my parents. It would take several months before I could make any purchases. I was in need of a raincoat and had picked one out while window shopping on Königstrasse. It was a fashionable looking black trench coat with epaulets. In my mind's eye I was already wearing it.

Jean invited me to have dinner with her and her husband, Richard. They rented a small apartment in a section of Stuttgart easily accessible by streetcar. So one night after work I accompanied Jean to her apartment. Richard was of medium height with a shock full of dark, curly hair. He had a peculiar sense of humor that was not easy for me to take in. He was Jewish, and although I didn't yet know all the details of what happened to Jews during Hitler's awful reign, I had heard enough to feel a measure of guilt.

Our conversation flowed naturally. Although Jean and Dick were several years older than me, educated and mature, they delighted in my youth and were interested in hearing my story of the war and after-war years.

When David, who preferred to be called 'Dave,' invited me on a date, I was speechless. My experience in the dating department had been zero. Dave kept looking at me, waiting for an answer. My emotions were on overdrive. Should I say yes? Would my parents approve? It was easy to read me because my feelings were mirrored in my face. After a long silence, Dave finally said, "I would like for you to come to Stuttgart on Saturday. We could have lunch and explore the city. I've had little opportunity to see some of the sights and it would be fun to have you join me."

When I told him that I would let him know after I spoke with my parents, his face registered disbelief. Being American, he found it difficult to understand why an eighteen-year old needed permission to go on a date, but I was glad to have this reprieve. On the way home I tried to unravel why I did not jump with joy. After all, here was this handsome, worldly young man showing an interest in me. One objection I had was his height. Dave towered over me by one foot. Flats were the fashion of the day, but even if heels would have added a couple of inches to my height, I would have to wear flats because of all the walking.

That evening I told my parents about Dave's invitation. This brought an instant frown from my father. "You want to go out with an American soldier!" After a long pause I heard a reluctant, "Go ahead, but we want to meet this young man before you agree to see him again."

The next day I told Dave that I accepted his invitation. I also asked if he would be willing to meet my family. He seemed to have no problem with that; he even welcomed the opportunity to visit a German home. It occurred to me how lonely these soldiers were in a foreign land, so far away from their families.

On Saturday I quivered with excitement and this drove my family crazy. I tried on various outfits, asking their opinion, but not heeding their advice. Thankfully, it promised to be a beautiful day. The sun shone in a bright blue sky with nary a cloud in sight. The bus ride into Stuttgart allowed me time to bring my shaking under control.

Dave greeted me at the bus stop with a huge smile. I was surprised to see him in civilian clothes. He wore khaki pants, a baby-blue Oxford shirt; a navy cardigan was casually draped across his shoulders. We headed for a nearby restaurant for lunch. What a treat. The last time I ate out was in New York. Dave knew a little German, but I was pleased to translate the menu for him. Conversation flowed with ease as Dave told me about his family in Michigan and his years at Princeton. I shared a little about my family's journey.

Content and well fed, we strolled down Königstrasse. Dave liked antiques and loved to peek in the windows of the antique stores we passed. Since my family lost all our possessions twice, I had no particular attachment to material things, and knew little about antiques, but was willing to learn.

Dave had read up on Stuttgart's history. We leisurely walked around the Schlossplatz, alive with flowers in full bloom. The hustle and bustle of people deep in conversation enlivened the area. When we reached the opera house, Dave remarked that one day soon, he would invite me to a performance. I told him how much I loved the ballet, in particular Swan Lake.

Before the day's end we stopped at Café Marquandt for coffee and cake. I had my favorite, a fruit tart. On the way to the bus stop Dave took my hand, which felt wonderful. We only had a few minutes before the bus pulled in and I was sad our date had come to an end. Dave kissed me on the cheek as I climbed onto the bus.

The next few weeks were filled with bliss. I looked forward to my days at work. On his next free weekend, I invited Dave to come and visit my family. His visit was a huge success. My sisters swooned in Dave's presence and seemed to have lost their voices, timidly shooting admiring glances in his direction. My father knew a few English words, but mostly I had to translate. Mutti served us coffee and cake and I could tell that she, too, was charmed.

I now had official permission to date. Sometimes I stayed in Stuttgart after work. Dave was not always free on weekends, as he had certain responsibilities at his base. Whenever he could get a weekend pass, he liked to travel with friends, particularly with Bill

Murphy, who also worked with us. This was good, as I didn't want to neglect my friend Adele. I often traveled on the same bus to and from work with her, a time for catching up.

The swimming pool opened at the end of May, a big event for the local populace. My sisters had been counting the days because much of their social life unfolded there. Young and old arrived with blankets, beach towels and some with chaise lounges, which they spread out on the expansive green lawn. An occasional umbrella brightened the landscape, although there was little need for one. It seldom got really hot. Large trees surrounded the pool, giving it privacy from nearby busy Autobahn. The pool itself was almost Olympic size; the water temperature never got comfortable, but Germans are hardy people.

My sister Bärbel belonged to the DLRG, the German Life Saving Association, a club that taught life saving techniques. She and many of her friends taught swimming lessons and watched out for the safety of all swimmers. Bärbel was proficient in the breast stroke and the crawl, but her strongest stroke was the butterfly.

Whenever I had no other plans I, too, would enjoy the pool activities. Everyone was fascinated with me because I had been in America; I guess I was a minor celebrity.

In July, my half-brother, Hannsjoachim, was getting married. Mutti and I planned to attend the wedding, my first one. I was glad that Aunt Olga had made me a pretty dress when I was in New York. It was simple, sleeveless and had a full skirt. The periwinkle color looked good on me. A thin gold belt added a little sparkle since I did not own jewelry. Mutti planned to wear a black taffeta dress with a short jacket she had inherited from America.

The wedding was to be in Melle, a city in Lower Saxony. We boarded a train in Stuttgart and prepared ourselves for a five-hour journey. We each had a book that entertained us when we were not talking or looking at the rapidly passing landscape.

Hannsjoachim's bride, Elisabeth, came from a large family, three brothers and two sisters. One of the brothers came to the station with Hannsjoachim to fetch us. We were guests of Elisabeth's aunt, Tillie, who owned a large house with several bedrooms. She was a war widow and now lived all by herself. It amazed me how one person could occupy so much space.

We had several hours before we needed to put in an appearance for the evening festivities.

I dressed in my full black skirt that flared out when I wore a crinoline underneath. A form-fitting blouse and wide red belt showed off my eighteen-inch waist, of which I was quite proud. A large crowd had already gathered in front of Elisabeth's house. We met so many people – cousins, aunts and uncles and friends. Their names and faces were a jumble in my head. Mutti was delighted when she spotted her cousin, Vinzent Ludwick, and his wife Meta, who had been so kind to me when I left for America. Onkel Vinzent gave me a big hug and told me he liked my new look. Mutti had not seen her cousin since before the war and they had much ground to cover.

On this night, we celebrated 'Polterabend', an old Germanic custom in which the night before the wedding the guests break porcelain to bring luck to the couple's marriage. An old adage, 'Scherben bringen Glück' (shards bring luck), was the motive for this unusual custom. No official invitation was extended. Friends and family members just showed up in front of the bride's house, armed with broken dishes and pottery. Glass was not allowed. The bride and groom had the chore of cleaning up the piles of broken dishes. This was to make them aware that they will have to work through difficult situations in life. A box with broken dishes sat in a corner for those who had not brought their own. I picked out a couple of plates with a colorful design, and enjoyed the thrill of seeing them break into many pieces when I hurled them to the ground.

In a small side yard, narrow wooden tables and benches had been set up. A cold buffet, beer and wine invited guests to help themselves. Red and white checkered table clothes covered the tables and an accordion player provided music. Elisabeth's brothers took me in tow and introduced me to friends and family. The atmosphere was one of laughter and happiness and although I was a stranger, I had a wonderful time.

The wedding was the next day in a Catholic church several hundred years old. The bride and groom were already man and wife, since they had a civil ceremony two days before, which is the law in Germany. I was part of the bridal party and walked in the procession on the arm of one of Elisabeth's brothers. Elisabeth was a beautiful bride and Hannsjoachim looked handsome in a tuxedo. The Catholic ceremony felt foreign to me, and yet I could appreciate the solemn rituals. Mutti was visibly moved and I noticed that she dabbed at her eyes with a handkerchief. I felt uncertain about what to do when people knelt on the fold-out benches and decided to just stay seated.

The reception took place in a local restaurant where some sixty people had gathered to celebrate. Food and drink were abundant. There were speeches and toasts and when a band began to play, I was grateful for the dancing lessons Vati had given us. I was thrilled when a handsome young man invited me to dance a waltz. This joyful event ended much too soon and before we knew it we were back home.

Dave and I took much pleasure in each other's company. But there was no place where we could have privacy. While the weather was still beautiful, we often walked in the forest. There we spread out a blanket and did some serious necking. Dave was very respectful of me, and since I knew almost nothing about sex, we avoided a deeper entanglement.

I decided to knit a pullover to give to Dave for Christmas. A knitting store in Stuttgart offered an assortment of wool in every shade of the rainbow. I selected a pattern, skeins of blue-grey wool, and the appropriate size knitting needles. Several years earlier I learned to knit in school and was confident that I could master the pattern. I spent every free moment sitting in the corner of our dining area knitting. In the beginning I made several mistakes and had to start all over. It took many hours to finish the pullover, but I did not count them.

I invited Dave to join me and my family for our Christmas Eve celebration, which would be so different from what he was used to in America. I was glad when he enjoyed our unusual Christmas Eve meal. During dinner I was on pins and needles, anxious to get started with our 'Bescherung' (the giving of gifts). I could barely contain my excitement, wondering how Dave would like my creation. Success! He loved the pullover, which fit him well, and the color complimented his eyes. Unfortunately, there was no room to put Dave up for the night so he caught the last bus back to Stuttgart.

On New Year's Eve Dave invited me to the Stuttgart Opera House to see "Die Fledermaus," an operetta composed by Johann Strauss. Beloved for its joyful music, the story is a farce and cause for much laughter. The audience was dressed in festive attire. Evening gowns and tuxedos were not worn where our seats would be. In peanut heaven, the audience dressed less formal. From the first strains of the overture I was transported to another world. My body wanted to dance and sway. During intermission many in the audience drank champagne, which was served in the lobby area, compliments of the opera house.

The performance ended by 11 p.m., allowing time for most to get home by midnight. Dave and I stopped in a restaurant for a bite to eat before I caught a late bus home. There were only four other passengers on the bus, a young couple who found themselves a seat way in the back, and two young men, who appeared to be slightly inebriated. I entertained myself by reviewing the delightful performance of Die Fledermaus. The melodious music was still vivid in my memory and I would have hummed, but didn't want to draw attention to myself.

Little did I know when I awoke on this first day of 1956, how many life-changing events it would bring. First, my parents finally agreed to get a telephone. Even before it was installed, Vati lectured us on its use. He wanted us to understand that in addition to the monthly charges, each outgoing phone call would incur an additional cost. I can still hear his voice as he attempted to teach us phone etiquette: "Keep your conversations short; only use the phone when absolutely necessary." On and on he went.

I immediately memorized our phone number, anxious to relay it to my friends. It was exciting that they could now get in touch with me. Mutti wrote to our brothers, encouraging them to call.

Once installed, the phone sat on a tea cart pushed against the wall. Its color was a disappointing black. The first time the phone rang we all jumped at the shrill sound. But soon the novelty wore off and it seemed like we had always owned a telephone.

In February I celebrated my 19th birthday. It fell on a Friday, a work day. A birthday card from my American aunts awaited me when I sat down to breakfast. It also contained a long letter from Aunt Alice. My breath almost stopped when I scanned the two pages. Tears began to flow freely down my face.

I knew that Aunt Olga was dealing with many health challenges, which she had always handled with great courage. Now, in addition to her diabetes, she had developed a heart condition. This forced her to take early retirement from her teaching position. Under the circumstances, my aunt wrote, they could not take on the responsibility of being my sponsors.

I was devastated! My dream of immigrating to America was crushed. I could hardly talk. I handed the letter to Mutti. A great silence hung over our breakfast table. No one knew what to say, so they hugged me.

Although I wanted to crawl back into bed and hide, I went to work. I was on automatic pilot and hardly registered my trip into the city. A large bouquet of flowers greeted me at my desk. They were from Dave. I valiantly tried to show my appreciation. Jean saw right away that something was amiss. When I shared my news, she comforted me with these words: "We'll just have to find you a new sponsor."

My coworkers threw me a party. In spite of my dark mood I couldn't help but smile. It felt wonderful to be celebrated.

A few days later Jean told me that she and Dick had discussed my situation and they wanted to be my sponsors. But this would have to wait until Dick got his discharge from the Army, which was still nine months away. He planned to finish his graduate studies at Columbia University in New York. For now my dream was on hold, but was still within reach.

As it happened, March stormed in like a lion. The weather was frigid and snow still covered the ground. We all longed for spring. But then there was the upcoming event of Uschi's confirmation, which brought a bit of excitement to our home. She would be confirmed at the Lutheran Church in Eltingen. My parents decided to celebrate this milestone by giving her a party.

All Uschi's clothes were hand-me-downs. When Mutti took her to Stuttgart to shop for a dress, she was ecstatic. Sadly, all who were being confirmed were required to wear black, which made me think of funerals. The dress Mutti and Uschi selected had a large white lace collar that framed her face and softened the drab look.

My friend Adele told me of her plan to be an "au pair" in France. She felt learning French would help her with her voice studies. It occurred to me that adding another language to my resume might also be advantageous for me.

And so I, too, wrote to the agency that placed "au pairs" in foreign countries. Soon several letters arrived in the mail. My parents had some knowledge of French and were able to read the various offers. I allowed myself to be guided by my father, who liked one particular family with six children. He thought their letter exuded much warmth. The lady of the house promised to give me French lessons on a daily basis. My main responsibility would be to be with the children. No house work was required, as they had a maid who took care of all the chores.

I spent several days reflecting on whether I wanted to undertake this new adventure. The idea of leaving my job, friends and family was a bit frightening. I had just begun to feel secure and found it difficult to give that up. As an "au pair" I would not receive a salary, only a small monthly allowance. No one could advise me, the decision had to be mine. And so I took another risk, and welcomed the unknown.

German law required that I allow three months to give my notice. I sought out Sgt. Sadek and informed him of my plans. He reluctantly accepted my resignation. My co-workers were sad to see me go. Jean was very encouraging and felt that adding French to my skills would definitely be a plus for my future. Dave was less enthusiastic; however, he was not far from receiving his discharge from the Army and planned to spend a year travelling in Europe. He reluctantly agreed that my plan had merit.

My last day of work was on June 30. Everyone wished me good luck. I promised to stay in touch with Dave and Jean. The goodbye from my family was more difficult. Again I approached the unknown, away from their support. But at least this time an ocean would not separate us. Vati reminded me that I was only a train ride away from home and could choose to return if things didn't work out.

The train slowly pulled out of the station. A window seat in a third class compartment reminded me how pivotal trains had been in my life. It was as if I was watching a movie: I'm seven when my 2nd grade class is evacuated because of the air raids, scared of what will await me at my destination. I am almost eight when we are forced to leave our home in Breslau in January of 1945 because the Russian Army is advancing, and I am sixteen when a train took me to Bremerhaven on my way to America. I could not help but wonder what fortune held in store for me this time.

My mother and father finally together again

Uschi in her confirmation dress 1956

Before one of our outings with Vati 1955

In front of Gerlingerstr. 38
Adele on left, Jean 2nd from right

Vati and me, with Sherry

Peter looking at his 3 sisters

Au Pair in France

No one had entered the compartment; I welcomed the solitude. My parents taught me a number of French phrases, which I had recorded in a small notebook. I repeated them out loud since no one could hear me, "Bonjour, Bonne Nuit, Au revoir, merci beaucoup, je ne comprend pas, comment ça va." I could even count up to ten.

It did not take long to reach the French border where customs officials boarded the train to check passports. Two good-looking young men in uniform opened the door to my compartment. They greeted me with a smile and a "Bonjour Mademoiselle," a phrase I would hear often in the months to come. I knew enough to show my passport, and shook my head when I thought they wanted to know if I had anything to declare.

The border stop lasted no more than thirty minutes. A handful of passengers climbed on board, but still, no one entered my compartment. Butterflies were settling in my stomach; I could have used some diversion.

The French landscape did not look much different from Germany and yet I was in a foreign country, a country whose language I did not know. When at last we pulled into Montreuil-sur-Barse, I grabbed my light suitcase and made my way to the exit door.

It did not take long before I saw a young woman headed my way. She was attractive, about 5'6", with auburn hair that was held back by two barrettes. Her smile was warm. She held out her hand, "Mademoiselle Grunwald?" I nodded, unable to come up with a reply. I was relieved to discover that Madame had some knowledge of German and for now no French was required on my part.

We walked to a parking lot where a dark blue station wagon was parked. Madame Devereaux told me that we had a thirty minute drive to the small village where the family lived. Not much was said on this short trip, but Madame looked at me often and smiled. She told me that the children were excited to meet me.

Montreuil-sur-Barse was truly a village. I was shocked when I observed one long road with no shops. Farmlands spread out on both sides. I learned later that there were only 276 inhabitants. We reached a fenced-in piece of property. This is where my home would be for who knew how long. The gate was open, revealing a sprawling farm house that must have been several hundred years old. It had two entrance doors and from the first, children came running to greet the car. Madame tried to calm them and commanded that they let me into the house. We entered a spacious kitchen with a low ceiling. A huge wooden table with many chairs sat in the center. There was also a massive side board.

Back against the wall, a stocky teenage girl stood defiantly, clutching a chubby baby boy whose arms strained towards his mother. This was Denise, the maid who took care of all the household chores and the cooking. Her beady eyes looked at me with suspicion and she barely managed a nod when Madame introduced us. She came from a nearby farm and was used to heavy work, which was evident when I saw her calloused hands. It would take some work on my part to make friends with her.

The children became noisier by the minute, each clamoring to be acknowledged. There were four girls and one boy. It took some effort to calm them. They were not satisfied until they had been introduced to me. Their names rattled around in my head. I didn't think they realized I could not understand a word they were saying. I shook their hands and smiled my prettiest smile for I did want them to like me.

The oldest girl was eight; her name was Victoria. She had been chosen to take me to my room, which was upstairs on the other side of the house. They all wanted to come along, but I was glad when Madame discouraged that.

Victoria and I made our way through a hall and up a short

flight of stairs. My room had an odd shape. It was not square or round. Sharp angles went every which way. Adjacent was the children's room. The room was furnished with a single bed covered with a colorful bedspread, a small narrow desk with a chair, and an armoire where I immediately hung up the few clothes I had packed. Victoria was helping me and I was glad that I could at least thank her in French.

On our return to the kitchen Madame asked the children to show me the outdoors before their father arrived home from work. I was impressed with the property that seemed to go on forever. It was like a park with beautiful trees, completely fenced in. The children ran ahead, inviting me to chase them. I made a weak attempt to run, but somehow could not get up enough speed to catch them. I was worn out from my trip and the excitement of being in France. Little Claire was only 2½ and her legs could not carry her as quickly. She took my hand and my heart melted when I felt her pudgy little fingers. Her smile was angelic. In the days to come, the park would become our playground when the weather was nice, a great way to entertain the children as we searched for treasures from nature.

When we got back, Monsieur Devereaux had arrived home from work. He was a lawyer and worked in a nearby town. He was tall and his relaxed features invited one to like him. His hair was curly and midnight black. He welcomed me to his home with a firm handshake and asked his wife to tell me in German that he hoped I would be happy with my stay in France.

The table had been set for dinner. The children each had their assigned seats and the grownups were spread among them so they could be of help. I got to sit next to little Claire and on my other side was François, who was four years old. The children were served water combined with concentrated fruit juice. The adults drank white wine in water glasses, mixed with seltzer water. I would rather have had some of the fruit juice, but I was expected to drink the wine. There was butter on the table and several baguettes of that wonderful French bread, which we tore off with our hands. Denise served the food and I was surprised that each course was eaten separately. First the vegetables, followed by pasta or potatoes, and the meat came last. In time, I adjusted to this new way of eating. Conversation around the table was lively, although I couldn't understand a thing being said.

After dinner, Madame asked that I join her as she prepared the baby for bed. We went to a small room next to the kitchen where the baby spent much of his time during the day. The baby's name was André, but he was simply referred to as "Bébé." Madame told me that I would only be responsible for the older children. I was disappointed that I wouldn't have the opportunity to tend to Bébé.

The children's bedtime was eight o'clock. All of us marched upstairs to help them prepare for this nightly ritual. The older children didn't require assistance, but needed to be reminded to brush their teeth and use the toilet. Their room was spacious, furnished with five beds and little else. If there were toys, I did not see them. There was much giggling and jumping going on and I wondered how long it would take for the kids to settle into their beds. Madame invited the children to join her in prayer and wonder of wonders, calm prevailed just like that. I learned that the French word for God is 'Dieu'.

I was now free to go to my room. There was nothing to do and I felt lost and lonely. Luckily, I had brought a couple of books and settled on my bed to read. There was still some light coming from the window close to my bed. I could hear whispers from next door, telling me that the children were not yet asleep. My eyes were heavy and I decided to put on my nightgown. The murmurs of the children and the creaking noises from the old house lulled me to sleep. This first night away from home was restless, filled with weird dreams.

Morning dawned. The chatter of children woke me. I was not sure what would be expected of me. Madame was already next door directing the children to get washed and dressed. When I entered the children's room, she told me that Victoria and Marie had to leave for school shortly and asked if I would please help the other children get dressed.

This gave me the opportunity to acquaint myself with Isabelle,

François and Claire. Isabelle was around five years old. She was the only one with blonde hair. It curled around her small face. She was a beautiful child, reminding me of a little fairy. Her bright blue eyes challenged me and I could see that we might butt heads in the future. François was charming and acted already like a miniature gentleman. He required no help with his wardrobe. Little Claire looked at me beseechingly when she tried to dress herself and I was more than happy to assist her. I made a game of it by asking the names of the different items of clothing. The children jumped at the chance to outdo each other in supplying the correct word. Thus I rapidly added to my limited vocabulary.

At breakfast the children were served hot milk and French bread spread with butter and jam. Denise offered me a cup of coffee, which I gladly accepted. Her demeanor was still on the sour side. I could hear the baby making sucking sounds as Madame fed him his bottle. All appeared calm.

Since it was a beautiful day I led the children outdoors and we continued our game of naming everything we saw. Across from the house was a small stable where a sheep lived. We went to meet this large furry animal. Much later I learned that he would be slaughtered in the fall to provide meat throughout the winter months. That made me sad. There were no other animals on the property, not even a cat.

We followed a path that led us to the end of the property, eventually winding back to the house. Midway down the path, a swing hanging from a gigantic tree moved gently in the breeze. Everyone wanted to get on at once. Since I couldn't say, "You'll each get a turn" in French, I simply pointed to them. Isabelle insisted on being first, naturally. She knew how to pump and I just had to get her started. Little Claire was less skilled.

It was getting close to lunch time and I guided my charges back to the house. The children's faces were flushed from being active and in the fresh air. They had definitely worked up an appetite. Lunch was served as soon as the two older girls returned from school. They ate a type of farina with fresh fruit. Madame and I had more French bread with cheese and cold cuts.

While the younger children took their afternoon nap I had my first French lesson with Madame. It took place at the kitchen table. She had purchased a French lesson book, which served as a guide. By now I had amassed quite a few nouns but lacked knowledge of verbs and adjectives. I found Madame to be a good teacher as we worked our way through the first chapter in the book.

My sole role was to entertain the children, not an easy task because of the wide range in their ages. Isabelle presented a particular challenge. She was a drama queen and mama's pet. When she did not get her way she pouted. She screamed at the top of her lungs when she had an innocent fall and accused her siblings of having pushed her. Something of that nature happened almost every day. I soon grew weary of her tantrums.

In time, my French lessons dwindled to two or three a week. Madame often had appointments with doctors or other dates she had to keep.

I was to have one free day a week; however, there was nothing for me to do. The village had no shops and I had no transportation to venture into another town. My store of books ran out. The children did not understand that I would not be available for them on my day off.

I shared my plight in letters I wrote to my family, to Dave and Jean. Dave was very sympathetic and supplied me with new reading material every two weeks. One day a large package arrived with a portable record player and a number of records. There was only one problem; I was not allowed to play it when the children were asleep, which was when I had free time.

In spite of my lack of French lessons my French improved with each day – thanks to a small dictionary I carried with me. I found it easy to converse with the children, but not when I spoke with Madame and Monsieur. They tried to engage me in conversation whenever possible, but I felt intimidated in their presence, afraid of making mistakes.

In late July school closed for six weeks. Victoria and Marie now joined us in our outdoor playtime. Victoria was quite good with her siblings. I found her presence helpful. I asked her to teach me

French songs and games. Since the children didn't understand German, I could not apply my large German repertoire. Victoria taught us games she and Marie played during recess at school. I also learned a number of simple French children's songs.

In August, Monsieur Devereaux took a two week vacation. The family planned a trip to the French Alps where they would rent a house. It would be a welcome change, a chance to see a different part of France. Denise stayed behind to look after the house and tend the sheep.

On the day of our departure our luggage was loaded on top of the station wagon. I had my doubts as to how we would all fit inside the car. Madame sat in front, holding the baby on her lap. Victoria, Marie and I sat in the back seat. The other three children made themselves comfortable in the open back area. Seat belts and car seats were not yet in vogue, putting fewer restrictions on the children, who could move around freely. Our destination was near Chamonix, the winter and summer playground of the rich and famous.

The next two weeks went by in a flash. The children loved being in a new environment. They anxiously explored the rented house, which was quite comfortable. Monsieur took us on daily outings to fairytale-like villages and towns. One day we rode a cable car, which offered a spectacular view of mountain ranges.

Monsieur also arranged daily hikes in nearby forests. He purchased walking canes for all of us, to the delight of the children, who wielded them like swords and poked each other. Monsieur taught them their proper use. Bébé rode on Monsieur's back in a sling; his chubby arms and legs were free to kick and he had the best view. We created quite a sight as we walked like a bunch of ducks on narrow paths.

I was sad when the time came for our return trip. The change of pace had been good for everyone.

When we arrived home, Denise greeted us at the door. Wonder of wonders—she was actually smiling. A stack of letters awaited me. It was evening before I had time to read them. The car needed to be unloaded, suitcases unpacked, children had to be fed.

It was late when I got to my room. With a deep sigh of relief I collapsed on my bed. I could not decide which letter to read first. My family won, and I read my father's type-written letter filled with news from home. He was an excellent writer. Next, I read Dave's letter. He wrote that his discharge was coming up in November and he planned to travel to Spain. A letter from Jean told me how she and Dick would soon return to the States. She wrote that they would begin sponsorship procedures as soon as they were settled and Jean had a job. That was exciting news! Adele's letter invited me to join her in Paris for a long weekend visit in October. What a wonderful idea!

The next day I looked for an opportunity to speak with Madame about my plans to visit Paris. I was surprised when she requested that I get a letter of permission from my parents. At first I was annoyed, but realized that Madame and Monsieur felt responsible for me and my safety. I could understand that.

I sent a letter to my father with the next mail and it was not long before a reply arrived. Vati and Mutt gave their permission; I breathed a sigh of relief.

In the beginning of September there was a sudden change in weather. Mornings were cool and the sun had lost some of its strength. Trees were changing color and dropping their leaves. I instructed the children to collect the most colorful ones. We connected them with thin sticks, creating garlands. I draped these around the children like sashes and also fashioned crowns for their heads. Thus decked out, we marched along the path, pretending to have a parade.

And so the days moved in an orderly fashion, one running into the other. My excitement grew when I turned my calendar over and it was October. Adele was expecting me on Friday, October 12, for three nights in Paris. She had made reservations in an inexpensive Pension (inn) located on the Left Bank.

On the day of my departure, Madame was kind enough to drive me to the train station. I boarded the train, confident that I could speak French well enough to get by. Paris was only two hours away. I was on pins and needles, excited about seeing the city that had been immortalized in films, books and music.

Paris had several train stations; mine was the Gare du Nord where Adele would meet me. I spotted her as soon as the train had stopped.

A feeling of excitement embraced me when I took my first step onto the streets of Paris. The late October sun bathed everything in a golden glow. A bus took us to our Pension, where an elderly woman checked me in at the front desk.

Adele and I were euphoric. The weather was mild; streets teemed with people of all ages. I listened to the French chatter all around us. We sought out one of the many cafés that seemed to spring forth on every street. Outdoor tables with wire chairs invited us to stop for coffee and a sweet. Here we caught up on each other's news and made plans on what to see during the next few days.

Adele shared with me that she would probably not stay in France for a whole year. This encouraged me to voice my own concern for the first time. I, too, was not happy and wanted to return to Germany some time before Christmas. For now, however, these thoughts were pushed aside. We were, after all, in Paris, the most beautiful and romantic city in the world.

Our funds were limited, but Adele knew just about every worthwhile landmark and many required no money. And we were young and used to walking. I was already in love with Paris as we began our tour by strolling down the Avenue des Champs-Élysées, where the famous Arc de Triomphe greeted us.

And so we continued our sightseeing tour in the next two days when we visited Notre Dame, located on the Ile de la Cité. This also brought us close to the famous river Seine, which divided Paris's Left and Right Bank. Booksellers, who displayed their wares in metal green boxes, stretched for miles on the Right Bank. The Eiffel Tower and Sacré-Cœur, which offered a magnificent view of the Paris skyline, were just a few of the attractions on our list.

Paris had beautiful parks and gardens where we stopped to eat our meager lunches of bread and cheese. Here, small wire chairs could be moved to any location, a great place for people watching. I was fascinated by the many well-dressed women who walked with pride, their heads held high. They were not all beautiful, but they had the sophistication that comes from living in a cosmopolitan city.

Sadly, our time was quickly coming to an end. We had seen all the major attractions, taken the pulse of this exciting city and our hunger to know Paris had been stilled. But we decided to take in one more event—one that filled me with awe.

A special exhibit of French Impressionists was taking place in a low-lying building located near the river Seine. I had become a fan of Renoir, Degas, Monet, and others ever since I was exposed to their art at the Metropolitan Museum in New York City. Even though our funds were nearly depleted, we managed to come up with the admission fee.

Speech left me when we entered a long, large room displaying the art of only Impressionists. I was in my glory as I walked from painting to painting. I recognized so many of them. It was like being with old friends. We took our time and viewed all the paintings several times. This had definitely been worth seeing and remains as one of the highlights of all we experienced.

Back at the farmhouse the children greeted me with joy. It warmed my heart to be so unconditionally loved. That evening during dinner hour I was delighted when Madame and Monsieur asked about my time in Paris. Everything was still so vivid in my mind. Even the children listened with rapture. They knew all about the Eiffel tower and wanted to know if I climbed to the top.

That evening I recalled my father's words, "You can always come back home if things don't work out." I wrote to my parents to let them know of my intention to return home sometime in December. Since confrontations made me feel uncomfortable, I searched for a way to soften the blow. After all, my French family thought I would spend a year with them. I fell asleep trying to figure out how and when to tell Madame and Monsieur of my decision.

In late October I finally approached Madame with my news! From her facial expression I knew she was not pleased. I did not want to tell her that I was miserable. Instead, I talked about how my plans to immigrate to America were materializing faster than I thought. When Monsieur heard about my decision that evening, he, too, looked troubled. They asked that the children not be told until shortly before my departure.

In November the sheep was slaughtered by a local farmer. I could not bear to watch. For some reason, the children were totally unaffected. Perhaps they knew from years past that this would be the sheep's fate. Much of the meat was placed in a large freezer and the farmer took whatever was left in payment for his services. One evening we had mutton for dinner. A smell I could barely stand permeated the kitchen. I did not want to eat this meal and practically choked on this foreign taste. In my mind's eye I saw the sad face of the sheep.

When I finally told the children that I would soon return to Germany they protested loudly. Their anguished faces made me feel terrible, but I knew that in time I would be forgotten. Madame had already put out feelers to find another au pair to replace me.

My last few days in France were somewhat strained. Another chapter in my life was coming to an end. I did not regret the time I spent with this French family. Although I was not fluent in French, the experience had helped me to learn the language well enough to build on this knowledge in the future.

Final Months in Stuttgart/Leonberg

I arrived back home in the middle of December. It was wonderful to see everyone, but it took a few days to acclimate myself to our tight quarters. The air was already filled with preparations for Christmas. A beautiful Advent wreath hung from the ceiling and I looked forward to the lighting of the candles on Sunday.

Although this was not the best time of year to find a job, I visited the Stuttgart employment office. They still had my records on file and I only filled out a couple of forms. After a short wait I was told that there was a position at Robinson Barracks with the 25th Base Post Office. I needed to go for a personal interview with a Captain Miller. The young woman who had previously helped me made the appointment. Captain Miller could meet with me in two days.

Robinson Barracks was one of the most scenic posts in Stuttgart, located on the Burgholzhof. It and the Grenadier housing area commanded a great view of the city. It also housed the largest PX in Europe, serving 32,000 Army personnel and civilians. A bus took me to Bad Cannstadt and from there I had to walk up a steep hill. I wondered how I would manage this trek during inclement weather. I timed myself and it took a good 15 minutes to reach the top. I was out of breath and in spite of the cold, I felt toasty warm. I scanned the many buildings, not sure where to go. Fortunately, I spotted a young soldier and asked for directions to the Base Post Office. He was heading there himself and invited me to follow him.

The Post Office was a huge warehouse-like space located in the basement of a large building. Here, enlisted men in fatigues were busy carting sacks of mail. I made my way to Captain Miller's office, located in a corner. Captain Miller had an open, friendly face and I liked how he greeted me with a warm smile and a firm handshake. He asked a number of questions about my background and explained what the job would entail. He marveled on how well I spoke English.

Captain Miller told me that this Post Office handled enormous amounts of mail, which was distributed to various locations in Germany. There were thirty enlisted men under his command, some were draftees and others had made the Army their career. Because of the volume of mail, many claims were made for lost or damaged packages and lost mail. Taking care of these matters would be my responsibility.

I was shown a tiny office, furnished with a desk, a typewriter, a filing cabinet, and shelves with many postal forms. With lots of noise coming from the large mail room, I found it difficult to see myself in this drab place. And yet, I needed the job and when it was offered to me, I accepted. Because of the upcoming Christmas holidays, Captain Miller suggested that I start work on January 2. That suited me well and I left the interview feeling glad that I would soon have an income.

With Christmas approaching there was the usual excitement in the air, but I was sad that I did not have the funds to purchase presents for my family. But then our celebration had never been about presents and that thought comforted me. My sisters were home from school and I was glad for their company. Adele was still in France and all my American friends had scattered in different directions. Loneliness was creeping into my bones.

My cousin Bodo came to celebrate New Year's Eve with us. He was like a breath of fresh air. Vati prepared a punch to help us usher in the New Year. As always, we had much fun when we poured the lead that was to tell us what lay ahead. Bodo was not familiar with this tradition and we showed him how to melt the small piece of led over a candle, and how to quickly drop it into the bowl of cold water. He was delighted when his piece produced the shape of a bird with open wings.

When my father served the punch, I was determined to get tipsy. I quickly drank several glasses of the good tasting concoction, but instead of getting high, I got violently sick before midnight. Mutti made me lie down. Everything was spinning around me. I was miserable and upset that I was missing the arrival of midnight. Everyone was sympathetic and I got a lot of attention, but before long I fell into a dreamless sleep.

On New Year's Day I received a lot of teasing about my escapade the night before. Vati felt and I agreed that I had learned a valuable lesson. I definitely did not ever want to feel that sick again. That afternoon I joined my family for a long walk. The fresh air revived me and I felt reborn. I looked forward to a new year of possibilities.

The next day my sisters returned to school, Vati left for his job and I embarked on my new adventure. It was still dark and very cold as I waited for the bus to take me to Stuttgart.

I reported to Captain Miller. He introduced me to Private Larry O'Brien, who had been covering the claims office for the past few weeks. He would show me the ropes. I liked Private O'Brien right away. He was nice looking and had a wonderful sense of humor. He asked that I call him by his first name.

My first day went by quickly. Larry was a good teacher. Before long I was familiar with the various forms that needed to be filled out for lost or damaged items. I learned from Larry that service men loved to send Hummel and Lladro figurines, as well as cuckoo clocks to their loved ones in the States. Many arrived broken because they had been poorly packed. When a claim was filled out, proof of purchase had to accompany it. There was a big backlog sitting in the inbox and we worked diligently to make a dent in the pile.

Throughout the day soldiers, as well as civilians, came to the office looking for packages that were shipped from the States. Outside the office was a small table with a chair where they could sit to fill out the necessary forms. On this, my first day, the hours went by swiftly. I had brought my lunch and Larry showed me a small mess hall where I could eat and have a cup of coffee. Larry joined me and we shared our histories. I learned that he was from Massachusetts and he only had one more year left on his tour of duty. I was surprised when five o'clock arrived. It had been a good day and I was confident I could handle this job with ease.

The next few weeks passed swiftly. I left for work in the dark and it was dark when I returned home. January weather was very cold. I wrapped myself like a mummy when I walked up the steep hill to Robinson Barracks. If I was lucky, a car stopped to give me a ride. Private Larry O'Brien was assigned to another position and I was now on my own. The job presented few pressures; there was tediousness to it, only broken when I had customers.

The foul language coming from the mailroom proved to be disturbing. I had not been exposed to such outbursts and attempted to close my ears when I heard offensive words. Many of the enlisted men flirted with me. My shyness only egged them on. Often soldiers would ask if they could take me on a date. I had broken my relationship with Dave when he left for Spain without wanting to commit himself. However, I found my best defense was to pretend that I was dating someone.

A surprise greeted me one day when I returned home from work. A four-legged animal had joined us in our crowded apartment. A breeder of Dachshunds was unable to sell this darling pup because he was born with a broken tail. The dog looked funny with his bent tail, but he did not seem to mind, and neither did we. His short fur was black and shiny; around his face were flecks of brown. After much discussion we named him Sherry. The chore of walking him was divided equally between all of us.

Sherry proved to be little trouble and brought us much joy. He was housebroken and rarely had an accident. My sisters and I vied for his affection by holding him on our laps. That was, until Vati reminded us that he was not a lap dog.

I received several letters from my friend Jean. She and Dick had found an apartment on the Upper West Side of New York. Dick was completing his studies at Columbia University and Jean had found a job in a lawyer's office. They had begun the process of taking on my sponsorship, and Jean was told that it would only take a few months. That was wonderful news.

My brother Peter had been assigned to the Government seat in

Bonn, where his duties included guarding government facilities. He had met many famous politicians and even shook the hand of Konrad Adenauer, who had been German Chancellor since 1949. Although Peter liked his assignment, he requested a transfer to Stuttgart to be closer to us.

His upcoming move prompted my parents to inquire about an attic room in our building, which currently stood empty. So when Peter's transfer was approved in March, he rented the attic room.

We actually saw very little of Peter. He often stayed in Stuttgart after work and came home late at night. He was very popular with the opposite sex and had a string of attractive young girls who adored him. Occasionally, we got to meet one when he brought her to his bachelor pad.

Spring was slow in coming. Trees and bushes were ready to burst their buds, but sunshine was lacking. Here and there a purple crocus pushed through the still cold earth, while tulips were just barely visible. Easter was late this year. Even Sherry had spring fever. He longingly sat by the balcony door, hoping to be let out. Finally bright blue skies and a few sunny days allowed Mother Nature to erupt in splendor.

One day I found an official looking envelope waiting for me when I returned from work. It was from the American Consulate in Munich, advising that my sponsorship papers had arrived. I was told to present myself at the Consulate for a personal interview and a medical examination. Munich was two hours away by train and I decided to take a vacation day in early May, hoping I could accomplish all in one day. I could not afford to stay in a hotel and knew no one in Munich where I could spend the night.

I contacted the Consulate by telephone and made an appointment for a Friday. On that morning I left our house at 5 a.m., first taking the bus to Stuttgart, and from there I boarded a train for Munich. I looked forward to seeing a little bit of this city, the beautiful capital of Bavaria.

The pulse of this large and bustling city embraced me as soon as I left the train station. Many of its citizens were in national costumes so typical of Bavaria. Lederhosen and dark green felt hats with feathers were worn by men; the women were decked out in colorful full skirts, white lace blouses with full sleeves and snug fitting fleece jackets. The Bavarian dialect bounced around my head, making me feel like I was in a foreign country.

The Consulate was located at Koeniginstrasse 5. I barely arrived in time for my appointment. A young Marine greeted me at the door. I was impressed by his crisp uniform and shiny black shoes, but thought how boring this assignment must be for him; standing by the door and greeting people all day. He directed me to the second floor where a receptionist told me to have a seat. It was not long before a young man came and shook my hand. He would conduct the interview before I saw the medical doctor.

There was no reason to be nervous, but I couldn't help my inner shaking. The interview was brief. I surrendered my passport, which would be returned to me with the entry visa to the United States. The folder with my application also held the sponsorship letter. The interviewer asked why I wanted to immigrate to the US. I told him of my stay in New York City, and how I fell in love with America, and was looking for a better future in the States.

I was relieved when I could hand over a large brown envelope holding my chest X-ray. This was my last hurdle to overcome. I was asked some embarrassing questions about my sexual practices. When I blushed, the doctor did not question me any further. He studied my chest X-ray, listened to my chest and looked in my throat and ears. I was relieved when the medical examination was over. I was told that I would be notified when my visa was granted.

It was almost 2 p.m. when I left the Consulate. I was hungry when I saw a small Imbiss Stube (snack bar). I treated myself to a delicious sausage on a crisp roll and a glass of apple juice. Thus fortified, I decided that I had time to see at least one sight of this beautiful city steeped in so much history.

Vati told me to try to visit the Marienplatz (St. Mary's Square), a historic square that formed the heart of Munich. I received directions from a passerby. It only took fifteen minutes to reach the square. I was awestruck by its size, the large column in the center was known as the column of St. Mary. The square was closed to traffic. Throngs of natives as well as tourists casually strolled to take in the sights. Stores offered a variety of local merchandise. Bavaria is famous for its woodcarvers and one store offered beautiful carvings at exorbitant prices.

I could hardly wait to watch the famous Glockenspiel (carillon), which played every few hours. A large crowd had already lined up, waiting for the three o'clock performance. It was my good fortune to stand next to a distinguished-looking elderly man who gladly shared his knowledge of what was about to occur. The Glockenspiel, which dated back to 1908, consisted of 43 bells and 32 life-size figures. When it chimed it re-enacted two stories from the 16th century.

It was time to return to the train station. Trains ran every hour on the hour and I was glad to catch the five o'clock one. It had been a full day and I gratefully sank into the plush seat as my train carried me back to Stuttgart. My eyes closed almost immediately and I dozed for the next couple of hours, dreaming of the Glockenspiel. It was late when I arrived in Stuttgart and I still needed to catch a bus to Leonberg.

My parents were awake when I arrived home, eagerly awaiting news about my day's adventures. I was so wound up that I had a hard time falling asleep. Luckily the next day was a Saturday and I hoped to sleep in.

July and August were unseasonably warm. People flocked to the swimming pool to stay cool. It was a great place to entertain the children who were on vacation for six weeks. The days when Germans would travel far and wide were not yet here, and vacations were spent close to home. Whenever I could, I spent a few hours at the pool with my sisters and their group of friends. The water had gotten warmer and even I ventured for a swim.

In late August a registered letter arrived from the American Consulate in Munich. It contained my passport with a stamped entrance visa to the United States. I should have jumped up and down with joy, but for some reason I did not. I thought it would be months before my visa was approved. This was happening much too quickly.

The arrival of my visa ushered in a period of confusion and doubt. The enormity of what leaving Germany would mean hit me hard. I was not ready to discuss any of this with my family. Instead I went on long lonely walks, mulling over my situation, the pros and cons of staying in Germany or leaving it permanently. I was scared.

It was clear that I had no future in Germany because of all that had happened to us since the end of World War II. I did not feel connected. Though I was with my family, my surroundings did not constitute "home" for me. America, on the other hand, offered untold possibilities.

My friend Adele had returned from France in February. We met often, either for musical Sunday afternoons, or after work when we stayed in Stuttgart to take in a movie. I shared my concerns with her. Like me, Adele had a dream and she was frustrated by the uncertainty of her future. She advised me not to rush into anything, to take my time, and so we bounced several ideas around.

First, I needed to save quite a bit of money before I could leave for New York. There was the expense of the flight and I needed enough funds to support myself until I found a job. The exchange rate from German Marks to U.S. Dollars was not exactly favorable. It would most likely take me the rest of the year before I could acquire the necessary cash.

Second, I was not ready to say goodbye to my family. The step I was taking would be life changing. Who knew how long it would be before I could come for a visit? And so a plan developed. I would wait until after my 21st birthday in February of 1958. That seemed a long time away. For now I could relax.

When this decision had been made something strange happened. I no longer viewed life in the same way. I had thoughts like: this is my last summer here, my last fall, and my last Christmas. Tears welled up in my eyes every time I thought of bidding goodbye to Germany and my family.

My parents were very patient with me. They did not press me about my "America" plans. I sensed how difficult it was for them to let me go. They knew that a brighter future beckoned, and yet they hated to see me go so far away.

Jean's letters were encouraging. She thought I could apply for a job at Columbia University, which would allow me to take night courses at no charge. Their General Studies program was well suited for individuals like me. I liked that idea a lot. In my mind's eye I already saw myself among students and professors.

Autumn was a time of change and transition; days had grown shorter. The woods across the road were bathed in vibrant colors as if an artist had painted them. Cooler days invited one to hike, a pastime Vati enjoyed so much on Sunday afternoons.

On October 7 my sister Bärbel celebrated her 17th birthday. Her special day fell on a Sunday that year, and we observed this landmark birthday with an extra special meal. In the afternoon our brother Peter joined us for coffee and birthday cake. Since we saw him rarely, his presence enlivened our circle. He shared fascinating stories from his duties as a policeman.

The movie "Lili" with Leslie Caron and Mel Ferrer was playing in Stuttgart. I saw it when it first came out in 1953 in New York. Bärbel had little opportunity to go to the movies and it gave me pleasure to treat her for her birthday. In Germany, all foreign movies are dubbed. I was always amused then I heard actors like John Wayne or Elizabeth Taylor speak in German. Thankfully the songs stayed in their original language. As had happened before, when we left the movie theater passersby stopped me and asked if knew that I looked like Leslie Caron.

An invitation to a party brought a ray of sunshine to the dreary month of November. I had formed a friendship with a young woman who had stopped by my office on several occasions. She was from Denmark, and married to a man who had made the United States Army his career. They were housed in an apartment on the base. Inga was petite, a natural blonde and she had a childlike quality about her. She giggled a lot and I adored her accent.

The party was to be on Friday, so I was able to go and help Inga right after work. I wore my black full skirt with a crinoline and a lacy white blouse.

Inga and her husband Paul had two small children, a three-year old boy named Tobias and an eighteen month-old girl by the name of Freja. It became quickly apparent that I could best be of help by entertaining the children. They were adorable and took to me immediately. We sat on the floor of their room as they showed off their favorite toys – dolls and trucks – and I felt in my element.

I finally met Inga's husband Paul. He was a Master Sergeant who had tours of duty in many foreign countries. He was quite handsome and I loved the way he adored his wife. Soon people began to arrive. Young couples who also lived on the base as well as several single men, and two German girls. I spotted Siggi, who used to work with me at my previous job. She also had a job at Robinson Barracks and I was surprised that we had not run into each other before this.

Inga put out a wonderful spread of food. There were salads, cold cuts, herring and smoked salmon, and a variety of breads. Beer and wine, as well as soft drinks, were set up on a separate table. I was hungry and fixed myself a plate of food. That was when I first noticed him.

Lanky and tall, he leaned against the wall across the room, dressed in a light brown herringbone blazer and khaki pants. He had an aura of aloofness about him, accented by his slicked-down hair. When his eyes met mine, I felt myself blush. He sauntered over to where I stood; hand outstretched and greeted me with, "Hi, I am Tucker Moore." The young man had some difficulty pronouncing my name, but after two tries he said it quite well.

Tucker beckoned me to sit on the couch. I was curious about his accent. He told me that he was from Muskogee, Oklahoma, and in a hushed voice remarked that he was with the CIC, making it sound mysterious. I laughed and told him I knew all about the CIC.

We talked about our families, our backgrounds and before I knew it the evening had come to an end. Tucker offered to drive me home. I hesitated, explaining that I lived a long way away. He laughed and said that America was a huge country and a thirty minute drive would be a piece of cake. I dreaded going home so late at night on the bus and gratefully accepted this generous offer.

A star-speckled sky greeted us as we walked towards the parking lot. It was freezing cold. I do not recall the make of the car or its color, I just remember it had a battered look and made a rattling noise. The roads were empty. We reached my house in record time. Tucker walked me to the door. He placed a kiss on my forehead and said, "Don't ever change." How romantic can you get!

I was not sure how I felt about beginning a new relationship, but I was curious to know more about this young man from Oklahoma. However, when we parted that evening, nothing was mentioned about meeting again.

I was charmed when Tucker showed up at the Base Post Office on Wednesday. No longer in civilian clothes, his Army uniform showed how slender he was. He wanted to take me to dinner and we settled on the coming Friday evening.

When I told my parents about Tucker, they had ambivalent feelings about my seeing another American soldier. They had been so fond of David and were disappointed when our relationship broke up. I made light of my upcoming dinner date and explained that I needed to get back into the dating scene. Vati cautioned me to be careful. He worried about me.

Tucker picked me up after work, saving me from the long hike down the hill. November weather was cold and damp; climbing into a heated car was a wonderful luxury. I knew of a charming restaurant on the way to Leonberg, where we could have a leisurely dinner without being rushed. It was also half way to my home where Tucker could drop me after our date.

The restaurant I picked was decorated in country style comfort. Shaded lamps gave off a soft glow to the nooks and crannies in which tables were set with embroidered linen table clothes. It gave me pleasure to translate the menu for Tucker, who had no German language skills. I learned that he loved German beer which went well with the local fare. I ordered hot tea to take away the evening chill.

We had much to share. I learned that Tucker had two brothers and an older sister who was married and had two children. He was in the middle of studying architecture at the university in Oklahoma City when he decided on the spur of the moment to pack up his car and drive to Washington, D.C. He did not explain what prompted this move. There, he first worked in the office of a congressman and later at a haberdashery, where he bought the blazer he wore the night we met. Because he was no longer in school, he was drafted into the Army.

After basic training Tucker began his tour of duty in Stuttgart. Like the other men I had met from the CIC, he loved being here, enjoying a carefree life. He, too, had traveled to many countries. He fell in love with Mallorca, an island off the coast of Spain, where he purchased a black beret, which he sported at every opportunity. I learned his tour of duty would end in May of 1958.

Now it was my turn. I talked a little about the trials my family endured as a result of the war, our time in East Germany and our escape to West Berlin. I briefly touched on my visit to New York, and how it changed my future. I also revealed my plans to immigrate to the United States during the early part of the New Year.

No one rushed us. This was a good thing. I think we both enjoyed learning more about each other. Tucker asked if he could see me again. When he dropped me off at my front door, we agreed to meet the following week.

The time arrived when Tucker had to meet my family. I invited him to our home on the the afternoon of the first Sunday of Advent. As always, a beautiful Advent wreath hung from the ceiling.

When Tucker arrived everyone was there to greet him, including my brother Peter, who tended to be critical of my dates. Peter seemed to think he was in charge and that I must seek his approval. I scoffed at that idea, and let him know this in no uncertain terms.

Since Tucker spoke not one word of German, things were a little awkward. But my sister Bärbel was studying English in school and welcomed the opportunity to engage him in conversation.

Most of the time I was the translator as my parents asked polite questions. We had coffee with home-baked Christmas cookies, after which Vati lit the Advent candle. I explained the meaning of Advent to Tucker, who was not familiar with this tradition.

After Tucker left I was anxious to know what everyone thought of him. My parents said that it was too soon to have an opinion; that it was impossible to know someone after meeting them just once. My sisters liked him. Peter made a few critical comments, which I ignored.

There was little to do in winter time. I met Tucker regularly for dinner and he invited me several times to see a movie at Robinson Barracks, where American movies were shown on weekends. I learned about Tucker's idol, Humphrey Bogart, and began to realize that he tried to emulate him. He often quoted from the movie Casablanca; "Here's looking at you kid," it was a favorite phrase of his. When I finally saw a picture with Humphrey Bogart I could see why Tucker wore his hair like he did.

The Christmas season was finally upon us. In Stuttgart a wonderful Christmas Market went on for several weeks. Many booths were set up near the Schlossplatz, each decorated in a special way. One evening Tucker and I took in this romantic scene. Lights were strung around each booth; the smell of sausages and mulled wine permeated the air. At different locations musicians played Christmas carols, and children's choirs filled the air with heavenly sounds. Each booth offered a different specialty. I was happy when I found several Christmas gifts for my family.

Christmas Eve fell on a Tuesday this year and I was off from work for three days. My mother was busy in the kitchen preparing our special Christmas Eve meal. I breathed in the heavenly odors, trying to store them in my memory bank for the future when I would be far away from home. My father was busy behind the closed door of our sitting room, decorating the Christmas tree. My sisters were whispering and giggling in the room we all shared. Each time I wanted to enter they yelled, "Do not come in." I had a feeling they were working on gifts for the family.

My brother Peter joined us in late afternoon. He carried a

shopping bag filled with gifts, warning us to not peek inside. We devoured our evening meal, savoring the unique flavor of this food that is only served once a year. My sisters cleared the table and I joined them to help with washing and drying the dishes.

The magic of Christmas Eve was again revealed when Vati opened the door to the room that had been locked for days. And there it stood; a perfectly grown evergreen lovingly decorated in silver by my father. The flames of the white live candles danced as if there was a breeze in the room. When we burst into our traditional Christmas song, I choked. I was unable to sing. Peter unceremoniously poked me in the ribs.

In Germany we have two holidays, called the first and second Christmas day. I invited Tucker to join us on the first. He arrived promptly at the appointed time, bearing gifts for all of us. There was a carton of cigarettes for my parents, who loved American cigarettes; bottles of cologne for my sisters; a bottle of Old Spice for my brother Peter; a beautiful silk scarf for me. Everyone was happy. Tucker was especially charming and it was obvious that he appreciated being in a private home on this important holiday.

This New Year's Eve took on a new meaning for me because it would usher in 1958, the year I planned to leave Germany. I opted to celebrate with my family. Tucker went to Paris with some of his buddies.

Remembering how I had gotten sick the previous year from drinking the punch, I vowed to be more careful this time. I still would have liked a little buzz, but sipped my glass slowly.

As always, the pouring of the lead was anticipated with glee by me and my sisters. I got to go first. When I poured the melted led into the bowl of cold water a bird formed with wings spread wide. This was an omen I could readily accept and understand. My sisters, however, fared not as well when their lead just disintegrated into many tiny pieces.

At midnight we opened the balcony door to listen to the church bells. Their sound carried over many miles, proclaiming the arrival of the New Year. I joined Vati when he retired to the sitting room to listen to Beethoven's Ninth Symphony broadcast on the radio.

We sat very still for almost an hour, letting the powerful music wash over us. I felt close to my father. I also felt connected with all humankind when I listened to the words of the final chorus which proclaimed joy and unity among all. I vowed to keep this tradition going in the years to come, wherever I might be.

January arrived bringing much snow fall. I finally purchased a pair of boots to keep my feet dry and warm. I realized it was time to inquire about air fares to New York, and visited a travel agency in Stuttgart located near the Hauptbahnhof.

I felt timid as I entered the large storefront where posters of foreign lands decorated every inch of wall space. A young woman greeted me. I told her that I needed to know how much it cost to fly to New York. I could see the doubt in her face, but I convinced her that I was immigrating to America and needed to make flight arrangements.

TWA was the airline that flew from Frankfurt to Stuttgart, and rates varied depending on the date of departure. Since I had not picked a date I vaguely inquired about a fare in the month of March. I was not sure that I would want to leave that soon and maybe I did not want to go at all. So I told the young woman that I would return as soon as I had a definite date in mind. Since March was not the season for travel to New York, there was no fear that flights would sell out.

That evening I sat with my parents and discussed my travel plans. I started by saying that I had decided to wait until my 21st birthday, which was coming up in February. Their sad looks brought me close to tears. I finally decided to depart in March, and for some reason picked March 21, a Friday. A decision had been made.

Time went more rapidly than I would have liked. I worked, paid for my flight to New York, wrote to my American aunts and Jean to let them know when I would be arriving in March, and gave my notice to Capt. Miller. He was not happy to lose me, but wished me well. Capt. Miller thought that I would have no problem finding a job in New York because of my excellent work ethic. He promised to write a letter of recommendation. I still had the one from Sgt.

Sadek. All this gave me confidence.

Toward the end of January Inga and Paul asked Tucker and me to join them on a long weekend trip to Berchtesgarden, a charming town located in the German Alps. Paul and Tucker wanted to visit Hitler's Eagle's Nest, which was located there. When I shared these plans with my father he frowned. I assured him that I would be sharing a room with Inga, and Tucker would bunk with Paul. It was almost laughable how my father still wanted to control my life. Soon I would be twenty-one, on my own in another country, with no one to watch over me.

As I packed a small bag for the trip to Berchtesgarden I wished that I had a sportier wardrobe. My winter coat would have to do. The Autobahn was close to my home and I was picked up early Saturday morning. I was surprised, but pleased, that Tucker wanted to sit in back with me. Paul could hardly wait to let loose on the Autobahn where certain sections allowed speeds up to 140 miles per hour. This frightened me. Tucker put a comforting arm around my shoulder and assured me that Paul was a safe and experienced driver. We held hands for most of the trip, which felt good.

Somewhere in Bavaria we left the Autobahn. Winding country roads took us through charming villages dotted with farm houses, many of which had beautiful murals on their exterior walls. Since it was winter, the flower boxes on the balconies were covered with evergreens.

Soon we reached Berchtesgarden, where we had reservations in a small Bed & Breakfast. The owners did not speak English and I was the translator. A rotund elderly man led us to our rooms. He spoke with a heavy Bavarian dialect, so I had to pay close attention to understand what he said. Our rooms were simple, but charming. Windows looked out on snow-covered mountains. The fluffy feather beds were inviting. A nap would be welcome, but our little group was anxious to explore the town.

Berchtesgaden is a picture-book village tucked against the sheer wall of the Bavarian Alps. Winding streets lined with pastel buildings, decorated with paintings, led us to the market place.

Stores offered wood carvings and Bavarian clothes. Cafes invited one to try their Bavarian specialties, as well as beer, Kaffee and Kuchen (coffee and pastries). We took a break from window shopping and entered one. Tucker and Paul ordered the famous Bavarian beer while Inga and I had coffee with a delicious pastry, which we chose from a display case.

After an enjoyable respite in the café, we headed for the Tourist Information Center where we found many brochures, both in German and English, and we picked up information on the Eagle's Nest and other tourist attractions. We took these back to our lodgings to make plans for the next two days. Everyone was of one mind: let's have an hour's rest before going out to dinner. Inga and I climbed into our cozy beds. I wanted to peruse the brochures, but my eyes closed quickly and I fell into a deep sleep for an hour or so.

It was dark when we met downstairs. Our host, Mr. Meier, recommended a restaurant for dinner and I tried to remember his directions as we departed our B&B. We had a 10 minute walk ahead of us. It was cold outside and I wrapped myself with my warm scarf. The ambiance and warmth of the restaurant welcomed us. We spent the next two hours enjoying good food, drink, and lively conversation. Our plan was to visit Hitler's Eagle's Nest the next day.

Late the next morning we boarded a bus to take us to the Eagle's Nest, so dubbed by the Americans. The Germans called it "D-House" (for dignitaries) or Kehlsteinhaus, the name of the mountain it sits on. The architect was Martin Bormann, who undertook this immense job in 1937. The deadline for completion was Hitler's 50th birthday on April 20, 1939.

Over 3,000 men worked day and night, winter and summer for 13 months. A road was blasted out of the mountainside and passed through five tunnels to get to the entrance. The house itself sat on the summit, at 6,017 feet. We learned from the brochure that Hitler entertained here, but seldom spent the night as he was claustrophobic. He had another residence nearby called the Berghof. Our tour guide divulged other intimate and historic tidbits, but I was not interested in hearing much about Hitler, who created so much havoc for the world. Tucker and Paul, however, could not get enough information.

Later we visited a nearby Salt Mine, and drove to the picturesque lake Königsee. The long weekend ended much too soon. It was a wonderful experience for me and a chance to get to know Tucker better.

My birthday fell on a Monday. I expected to be awakened by ringing bells – after all, I was turning twenty-one. Nothing happened, I was still the same. Since my mother's birthday followed three days after mine, my family decided to celebrate that coming weekend. That was fine with me, since Tucker had asked to take me out for dinner on my birthday. We met near the Hauptbahnhof in Stuttgart and strolled down Koenigstrasse until we came to a restaurant of our liking.

During dinner, Tucker handed me a small box wrapped in deep blue paper, adorned with a silver bow. What might the box contain? I was curious, but took my time opening the gift. The box held a beautiful ring – white gold with a blue pearl and tiny diamond chips on the side. When I asked Tucker the meaning of this ring he said, "It is whatever you want it to be." Not a very satisfactory answer, but I did not want to press him further. The ring was exquisite and I loved it. I would ponder its meaning later.

Mutti invited Tante Fee and Onkel Heinz to help celebrate our birthdays on Sunday. She felt it might be the last time I got to see them before departing for the United States. We gathered for coffee and cake in the afternoon and Mutti also prepared a cold supper. My aunt and uncle presented me with a beautiful book about Stuttgart.

There was one more event in February I wanted to enjoy – Fasching (Carnival). Pre-Lenten festivities were celebrated in grand style in mostly the predominant Catholic regions. The Rhineland had its Karneval; Austria, Bavaria and Berlin called it Fasching. It began in some regions on the 11th of November at 11:11 p.m., or on Three Kings Day, January 7.

Parties, celebrations and parades came alive on this last

weekend before Ash Wednesday. Carnival had been celebrated for hundreds of years and stemmed from various beliefs and needs, providing a festive season of food and fun before the fasting Lenten season began.

On this Shrove Tuesday I decided to take a vacation day so I could join my sisters at the Leonberg Marktplatz (market square), where children and adults had gathered wearing colorful costumes. There were witches, clowns, princesses, little Red Riding Hoods and some devils. A parade was planned for later in the day. Farm stands offered hot cider and Berliner Pfannkuchen (donuts). Everyone wanted to indulge in silliness and laughter before the arrival of Ash Wednesday, which ushered in forty days of somberness.

March brought us a week of freezing weather. Our windows were covered with ice and our small stove barely managed to provide sufficient heat. Sherry was snuggled in his dog bed and refused to go out for his morning walk. My family huddled around the breakfast table, thankful for cups of hot tea. Mutti warned us to wrap scarves around our heads to prevent frostbite. I left for work as late as possible, but bus motors would not start and there were delays. I felt like I was in Siberia as I hiked up the hill to Robinson Barracks. I had lost all feeling in my hands and toes. It took a while to defrost when I got to the office. Spring was only three weeks away, but that seemed like an eternity.

March 14 was my last day of work. Many of the soldiers I had gotten to know, and customers of the Post Office, came to say goodbye to me. They all promised to look me up if they ever got to New York. Capt. Miller invited me for a farewell lunch. We drove down the hill to a nearby restaurant. During lunch I learned a little about his life in the United States, his family in Dearborn, Michigan, and how much he longed to be home. I had the feeling that he was jealous of my impending trip to America. He had written me a glowing letter of recommendation.

During my last week with my family I went from feeling euphoric to being down in the dumps. I was excited in one way, but fearful of what the future would hold. During family dinners our conversation was kept light. No one wanted to talk about my departure.

It did not take much to prepare for my trip. I only had my small wardrobe to pack. There were no trinkets and memorabilia to take, other than the book my aunt and uncle had given me. I met Adele one evening after she got home from work. She was encouraging and thought that I would have a fabulous future in America. We promised to write to each other. Her friendship had meant so much to me.

Tucker offered to drive me to the Frankfurt airport, which was a 2½ hour drive from Leonberg. I was grateful that I would not have to take several trains. We had seen little of each other these past two weeks, but had spoken on the phone.

And so the time had come. Mutti helped me pack and we both shed tears, wiped away quickly. My final dinner with my family was not a joyous one. The last farewell loomed large and we found it difficult to make conversation. Only Peter was bubbly when he arrived, just as we were finishing dinner. As always he had much brotherly advice to give me. I was touched when he presented me with a gift, a gold ring with a Topaz stone.

Before I went to bed, Vati called me to the sitting room. There he presented me with a small volume of poems by Johann Wolfgang von Goethe. It was one of the two volumes that accompanied him all the way to Russia, when he was taken prisoner of war. I was deeply touched and told him that I would treasure it always.

I was surprised that I could sleep. After a dreamless night my family and I sat down to one last breakfast. It was time to hug my father and sisters for the last time and tears flowed freely. Even my father's eyes were moist. I told my sisters that they must come to see me in America and that seemed to comfort them for now.

Only Mutti and I remained. She busied herself with the breakfast dishes. She was crying. Our goodbye would be painful. It was nearly 8 a.m. and Tucker was due any moment. I took one last look around the apartment, breathing in the familiar smells of my family. I cuddled Sherry for the last time. Mutti helped carry my heavy suitcase down the stairs. We held each other tight. Neither of us wanted to let go. Tucker lightly honked the horn, which took us out of our reverie. He had already put my suitcase in the trunk. I climbed into the front seat. Mutti and I waved for as long as we could see each other.

I sobbed for the next thirty minutes. Tucker did not interfere or try to comfort me. I used every last Kleenex. It was time to cease my tears. I took a deep breath and sat up straight. I was ready to begin my journey.

Most of our trip to the airport was on the Autobahn. Time passed quickly. Tucker and I talked about what lay ahead for me. We agreed to write to each other as soon as I had an address; I did not plan to stay long with Jean and Dick. Tucker would get his discharge in May. He thought he could arrange to be discharged in New Jersey. Our future was unspoken, but we definitely planned to connect once he was back in the States.

The Frankfurt airport was large and busy. I asked Tucker to let me out so he could turn around and drive right back to Stuttgart. It would be easier if I began this journey on my own. We hugged and kissed. Before I knew it his car was gone. I stood quietly for a moment, undecided where to go. Once inside I asked for directions to the TWA counter. Check-in went seamlessly. I had several hours before boarding my flight and wandered through the many shops. I even splurged and stopped at one of the kiosks for a cup of coffee and Danish, my comfort food for now. I felt so lonely.

Passport control and the security check were next. A small group had already assembled at my gate. I tried to discern whether they were German, American or of another nationality. The boarding process began. The plane was only half full and no one came to sit next to me. It was wonderful to be able to spread out my few belongings.

Young, attractive stewardesses scuttled through the narrow aisles handing out pillows, blankets and a small pouch containing all kinds of goodies. Another stewardess brought newspapers and magazines. This was my second time on an airplane. The one I took in 1953 from West Berlin to the West Zone of Germany was not pleasant because of turbulence. I also reflected on my first trip to America over three years ago, which was by boat and took twelve days. This time I would reach my destination in less than twelve hours. No time to make that adjustment of going from one continent to the next.

Takeoff was smooth. The captain came on the loudspeaker and gave us details about the flight. There would be a layover in London for refueling and the taking on of more passengers. Once we were in the air I felt like I was in no-man's land. I didn't want to think about anything – not the past, nor the future. I busied myself perusing newspapers and magazines. We were offered some light refreshments; dinner would be served after we left London.

When we landed a few passengers boarded; I was pleased that I retained the empty seat next to me. Our ninety minute layover allowed us to leave the plane to stretch our legs. I picked up British accents, which I found quite charming. Once we were in the air again, to pass the time I put on earphones and listened to music. From time to time I dozed thinking, 'New York here I come. Are you ready for me?'

When the Captain announced our imminent arrival in New York I was in a deep sleep. Excited voices, in both German and English, brought me back to reality. I organized my belongings, checked my passport and perused the customs form to make sure everything was filled out correctly. I had nothing to declare. A heavy cloud cover prevented me from seeing the New York skyline.

Finding Home - New York

Jean was meeting me at the airport. My flight arrived on time and I was grateful that Jean would not have a long wait. My stomach was queasy, probably from excitement. The captain managed a smooth landing and all the passengers applauded.

The hustle and bustle of the large terminal made me feel uneasy. I was not sure what to do next. Large signs pointed to passport control. When in doubt just follow the crowd. There were long lines in front of cubicles where uniformed men examined everyone's passport. My inspector was a young man. He greeted me with, "Welcome to America."

It took a while to find the carousel for my flight where I would collect my suitcase. A continuous flow of bags tumbled out of the chute and landed with a thud on the quickly moving conveyer belt. I was relieved when I spotted my suitcase and dragged it off with some difficulty. I had already secured a cart. Bags in tow, I got in line for the customs officials. Some people had several large suitcases. I noticed many had to open these for inspection. When it was my turn I handed over the customs form. When asked if I had anything to declare I just shook my head.

Large double doors covered with white film led to the airport. I spotted Jean's welcoming face in the crowd. Together we pushed the cart outside where I waited as Jean went to fetch the car. It was nearly dark. Airport traffic was heavy. Police waved cars on, allowing them only to stop if their passengers were already waiting. Jean pulled up in a beige Chevrolet. We quickly loaded my suitcase into the trunk and off we went.

It was rush hour and Jean warned me that the going would be slow, but this did not matter to me. I needed time to adjust to being earthbound and on a new continent. Jean and I had much to catch up on, and time flew.

Her apartment was located on the upper West side on 83rd Street, close to Broadway. Parking was a problem in New York City. After circling around we could not find an available spot close to her building. Jean double parked, and we unloaded my suitcase. I waited for her while she hunted for a parking space. The west side of Manhattan was unfamiliar to me—not an area I had frequented during my previous visit to New York. Many of the apartment buildings were six stories high. There was no elevator in Jean's building. We struggled to get my suitcase to the third floor.

Dick was waiting for us and greeted me with a big bear hug. Their apartment had a strange layout. A quick tour revealed a sparsely furnished living room, a small windowless kitchen, and a bathroom with a claw foot bathtub surrounded by a shower curtain. To get to their bedroom one had to pass through the kitchen. I would be sleeping on the living room couch.

Because of the six-hour time difference, I was fading quickly, but before I went to sleep Dick told me that he would go to Columbia University in the morning to study in one of their libraries. He offered to show me around the campus. Both Jean and Dick felt that Columbia might offer me a job opportunity.

The next day, Saturday, Jean was off from work so she joined us. We took the subway to 116th Street. I got my first view of Columbia as soon as we came up the stairs from the subway and crossed Broadway. Dick explained some of Columbia's history. He pointed out the majestic building of the Low Library, completed in 1897. Wide stairs led to the building, which now housed Administrative offices. In front, the Low Plaza reminded me of a beehive. Students were busily crossing the campus. Dick left it to Jean to give me a tour of the school. I soaked up the atmosphere of this prestigious university and college, the oldest institution of higher learning in the state of New York.

I had never seen so many good-looking young men in one spot. Jean told me that Columbia College was an all-boys school, while girls attended Barnard College, located across the street. We toured the various buildings, each housing a different specialty. We peeked into St. Paul's Chapel, which loomed large in university life. We also stopped a student to get directions to the employment office. I filed its location in my memory bank so I would be able to find it on Monday.

Jean also took me to Riverside Park, a four mile stretch of land between the Hudson River and Riverside Drive. Here row after row of benches invited one to sit and enjoy nature in a big city. The trees were still bare, but I was thrilled when I spotted a forsythia bush already in bloom, a reminder that spring was not far away.

On Sunday I had made a date to see my aunts for lunch. The 79th Street cross-town bus would take me close to 3rd Avenue. I could hardly believe my eyes when I reached my destination. The elevated subway on 3rd Avenue was gone. The ugly structure had been removed, opening up the Avenue to light. I very much approved of this change.

I made my way to the familiar white double doors of 205 East 82nd Street. My aunt "buzzed" me in. Aunt Alice was visibly moved when she opened the door to their apartment. She had changed little, but not so Aunt Olga. Aunt Olga looked frail and it was evident that she was not well. But her smile was the same when she embraced me. We sat down to eat a lunch of cold cuts and rolls, coleslaw and potato salad. This scene was so familiar from when I lived with them.

My aunts bombarded me with questions. They wanted a detailed account of Germany, my family as well as the Haase family. I shared my plan to apply for a job at Columbia University. When we said goodbye they asked that I visit them at least once a week and I was glad to promise that. Without them I would not be in New York, forging a new future.

On Monday morning, anxious to present myself at the Columbia Employment Office, I rode the subway with Dick who had an early class. He pointed me in the right direction when we got to the campus. A receptionist handed me an application that was several pages long. I filled it out and handed it to her with my two letters of recommendation. It did not take long before I was called into the office of the woman in charge. She introduced herself as Miss Engle. There was a suspenseful silence while she studied my application and read the letters of recommendation. When she finally looked up, she smiled and said that she thought I would make a good employee. She was impressed by my English and did not believe I had only been in the country for a few days. She also felt that my German and knowledge of French would be an asset.

Miss Engle searched a large file and pulled out several forms. "Oh, this might be a fit for you," she said. "There is an opening in the Columbia College Housing Office. Let me make a call to see if I can set up an appointment for you."

I crossed my fingers and silently affirmed that this might be the job opportunity I was seeking. The appointment was made for Wednesday at 11 a.m. I would be meeting with a Mrs. Ginger. Miss Engle gave me directions and wished me good luck. She also mentioned that I would need to apply for a Green Card in order to work. That was news to me.

I was on a high when I left Columbia and could hardly wait to share my good news with Jean and Dick. But that would have to wait until evening. Wednesday couldn't come soon enough. I was extremely nervous about the interview, but Jean told me to just be myself. She was already convinced that I would get the job. Wish that I could be that confident!

Mrs. Ginger at the Housing Office was a young woman, recently married, and I felt an instant connection with her. She explained the job to me. Columbia College had several residence halls, and this office handled all the room assignments, the dining hall program, processed the mail students received, and took care of all the student's needs. There were two other employees and I would make the third. The salary was $65.00 a week, and for the first year I would have one week vacation. That stunned me. In Germany everyone gets at least four weeks and some even have six weeks. Five paid holidays and four sick days were part of this package. An added benefit was the School of General Studies, where I could take courses without charge. I might yet get an education.

Mrs. Ginger appeared to like me and was impressed with my

letters of recommendation. She said that she was interviewing several more applicants, but hoped to make a decision within the next week.

After my interview I lingered out in the large hall. I loved seeing so many handsome young men, so close to my age. They were in the process of picking up mail, or had other business to conduct. I spotted a large bulletin board on one wall, displaying flyers about lectures and events, as well as personal advertisements.

A notice for a furnished room piqued my interest. It did not give an address, only a phone number, which I wrote down. Later that day I called the number and a female voice answered. The room was still available. The lady introduced herself as Mrs. Winter and she invited me to come see the room the next day at 2 p.m. The location was at the corner of 113th Street and Amsterdam Avenue, only three blocks from Columbia.

Jean and Dick were impressed with all I had accomplished in just two days. They helped me find the right office where I could apply for a Green card. That was on my agenda for later in the week. For now, I went to investigate the furnished room.

Mrs. Winter lived on the 14th floor. I was transported to another era when I entered the apartment. The furnishings reminded me of Victorian times: settees with large, bright flowers, tables and chairs with curved legs, and lots of lace on every available surface.

The living room was on a raised platform and very bright because of several large windows. The small kitchen was just big enough for one person. I would have kitchen privileges. The room for rent was a good size – it had a large bed with a lovely cover, a dresser, a comfortable looking chair, and a small desk in one corner. The built-in closet was huge. What a luxury! I couldn't help but think of the room I had shared with my sisters, which was half the size.

Mrs. Winter was a widow in her seventies. She had a full head of white hair that was swept up into a French twist and she was several inches taller than me. Her sweet smile endeared her to me.

Having German ancestors, she liked that I was German, and invited me to sit with her in her living room. She asked me many questions. I learned that the rent would be $60.00 a month with a month's rent as a security deposit. I explained that I was in the process of getting a job and wondered if she could hold the room for one week. She was agreeable and we parted on good terms, but not before Mrs. Winter advised me that she did not permit male visitors.

During the next few days I could think of nothing else but getting the job. On Friday Mrs. Ginger called and asked me to come by that afternoon. I was overjoyed. This time she gave me a tour of the office and introduced me to two other young women who worked there. One had an accent and I later learned that she was from Russia. I got the job. I could begin work on April1, just a few days away.

That evening I celebrated with Jean and Dick and called my aunts to tell them the good news. However, there was the small matter of money. I didn't have enough to put down a deposit on the furnished room. When I had the courage to ask my aunts for a loan, they willingly agreed to help me. I quickly made arrangements with Mrs. Winter, who agreed that I could move in on April 1.

It all seemed unreal. In less than ten days I had managed to find a job and a furnished room. After I took my deposit to Mrs. Winter I strolled up and down Amsterdam Avenue to acquaint myself with the neighborhood. My mind was on overdrive. I knew I was not the first immigrant to come to New York City, but when I reflected on the big chance I had taken, I felt an intense pain in my soul, a feeling of mourning – Weltschmerz. For just a moment I wanted to turn back; I longed for my family.

And then I spotted the Cathedral of Saint John the Divine. It called to me. When I entered into the sacredness of this beautiful Cathedral, still a work in progress, I felt a stillness I had never experienced. There was no one within. I sat down in one of the pews and beseeched whoever was in charge to help guide me. Time stood still. After a long interval, an incredible peace came over me. This beautiful sanctuary gave me courage and confidence. I knew at that moment that I would handle whatever lay ahead. My future would unfold in wondrous ways – America and its people would embrace me with loving arms. I had come home.

ACKNOWLEDGEMENTS

My Memoir had lain dormant for many years. Without the encouragement of family and friends it would simply have remained a dream without ever coming to fruition.

Life does move in mysterious ways. When I met Sunny Fader, a writer who offered to coach me and Pat Yochim, who was also attempting to write a short memoir, this book became a possibility. Sunny gave us confidence and she believed that we had a story to tell. Her devotion and generous giving of her time was unprecedented. I had no writing training. Sunny had her work cut out for her. Words cannot express the gratitude I feel.

I also would like to thank my sisters; Bärbel Collins and Uschi Ilka who helped jog my memory. Bärbel tirelessly read my early drafts and encouraged me when I wanted to give up. I'm deeply indebted to her.

Thank you to my early readers, Joan Kindy and Mary Carlson. Your input was much appreciated. I also thank my son Robert and his wife Allison, who encouraged me to go for it.

Before I even entertained the idea of a book, my book club friends listened to my story. They were deeply touched and urged me to keep writing. That was over eight years ago. So thank you, dear friends.

I am also grateful to John Rehg of Soul Attitude Press, who fashioned my story into a book. His expertise, advice and support are deeply appreciated.